In loving memory, to my father,

Leon J. Salter, a genuinely crosscultural person.

Brenda

———

To Ronald V. Myers Sr., Nina Lau Branson,

Pedro Aviles, Peter Cha and Brenda Salter McNeil,

dear friends and mentors on the racial justice journey

Rick

CONTENTS

FOREWORD

From a historical perspective, Sam Hines, Tom Skinner and I were reconciliation's first generation of pioneer evangelicals in the early 1960s. In the 1990s, Spencer Perkins and Chris Rice, Raleigh Washington and Glen Kehrein, Bill McCartney and others pushed reconciliation into the evangelical mainstream. Now, in this groundbreaking book, Brenda Salter McNeil and Rick Richardson are taking the reconciliation and justice movement to an even higher plain.

During much of the history of the Christian church, the Holy Spirit and the kingdom of God have been tragically divorced. This separation has allowed many Euro-American Christians to engage in ethnocentrism and oppression against ethnic groups. In *The Heart of Racial Justice*, the authors have essentially remarried the Spirit and the kingdom. Only the Holy Spirit can give us the power and wisdom to incarnate the kingdom of God here on earth. Only the Holy Spirit can heal the wounds of racism and empower us to do justice. This book holistically blends the Holy Spirit, the kingdom, justice and reconciliation, bringing together the concepts have been long separated.

I congratulate InterVarsity Christian Fellowship for leading the way among Christian organizations in wrestling with ethnic and diversity issues. I remember when Pete Hammond and I began this process of wrestling with these issues in Mississippi in the late 1970s. It was then that the InterVarsity board of directors made reconciliation a priority. In large measure this book reflects twenty-five years of struggle and success by InterVarsity.

The Heart of Racial Justice is deeply rooted in the gospel. This is the essence of racial, economic and social justice. God has made us stewards of the earth, and it is unfortunate that the Christian church has never quite understood what Paul meant when he said, "Now all things are of God, who has reconciled us to Himself through Jesus Christ, and has given us the ministry of reconciliation" (2 Corinthians 5:18 NKJV). We must stop reading only one dimension of meaning in that verse and embrace the two-dimensional perspective that leads us to reconcile not only with God but with one another, thus enriching our lives for the kingdom of God.

Promise Keepers, led by Bill McCartney, was the first attempt in my lifetime to massively present reconciliation as a blueprint for proclaiming the gospel. When Jesus said "By this all will know that you are My disciples, if you have love for one another" (John 13:35 NKJV), he was basing our love for each other as one of the determining factors for us becoming new creatures. Paul explains, "If anyone is in Christ, he is a new creation; the old has gone, the new has come!" (2 Corinthians 5:17 NIV). I thank Rick and Brenda for their work at clarifying this issue in these pages.

It is sad that in an enlightened world the Christian church even needs to deal with these issues today. Racial reconciliation has not been adequately addressed within the body of Christ. What Rick and Brenda do in this biblically grounded book is to make reconciliation practical through the example of their friendship, reflecting on those who have gone on before them and building on (and appreciating) what each one has to offer. I highly recommend that you take time to read *The Heart of Racial Justice*. It is a blueprint for the Christian church. We at the Christian Community Development Association (CCDA) want to make this one of our handbooks for the CCDA movement, because we view reconciliation as a practical reality that intersects all areas of our lives

All of this is from God who has reconciled us to himself and given us the ministry of reconciliation. Brenda and Rick have given us a challenge. I pray that all who read this book, especially those in the body of Christ, will take the challenge and become the next great generation of loving reconcilers!

John M. Perkins

ACKNOWLEDGMENTS

We are deeply aware that this book comes out of long years in dialogue and community with many friends and partners. We stand on the shoulders of many who have gone before us. We wish we could name and honor you all. Hopefully, many of you will see yourselves on the following pages, and know we are deeply grateful.

This book would never have seen the light of day without the belief in us that our editors at IVP have shown. To Cindy Bunch, Ruth Goring and Bob Fryling: Thanks! Cindy and Ruth, your editorial expertise made this book so much better. Thanks to Jim Bell for his helpful suggestions on the title. Thanks also to Ruth Haley Barton, who has held this book in her heart and prayerfully journeyed with us the whole way.

Words cannot express our love and appreciation for the many partners in InterVarsity Christian Fellowship who have worked with us, wept with us and worshiped with us as together we sought God's multiethnic kingdom of justice and love. Thanks too to the Urbana leadership team for inviting us to minister our insights at Urbana Convention seminars and sessions.

And thanks to J. Derek, Omari and Mia McNeil and MaryKay, Chris, Steve and Colby Richardson for your support and suggestions. Without your love and belief in us, and without your partnership in the racial justice journey, this book, and the convictions and ministries that lie behind it, would never have been possible.

INTRODUCTION

We have longed for racial justice, built on reconciled relationships, for years. We believe that healing people and nations is the need of the hour. We began our ministry together on the college campuses of urban Chicago in the late 1980s. We taught together about reconciliation and justice. Then we prayed for people in our multiethnic gatherings and conferences. We prayed in the power of the Spirit, trusting God to heal people and to begin to heal our city, and we saw God work in some amazing ways. That citywide urban campus ministry was the beginning for us of a journey toward peace with justice.

We have both experienced the power of reconciled relationships. Our lives would be quite different if we had stayed within our own ethnic circles. We appreciate a breadth of music, culture, art, relational approaches, worship styles and social perspectives that have enriched our lives immeasurably.

We have also experienced the pain of racial division and too many superficial and unsatisfying attempts to bridge the racial divide. Well-meaning people, including the two of us at points, have hurt others unintentionally. We have learned it is no easy thing to be reconciled and to work together for peace with justice. White people like Rick often want relationships but not justice, because justice involves painful social change. African Americans and other people of color, like Brenda, have become very tired of superficial relationships that don't lead to social change. Some people of color have even despaired and don't want to engage in the hard work of reconciled relationships until they have proof that those relationships will seek more than just warm feelings. In this book we want to get beyond the impasse. We seek peace with justice, and nothing less.

We have had victories in our work for peace with justice, and we have had discouraging defeats; you will read about both in the chapters to come. Through it all, we have experienced that God is powerfully at work in our day to heal people and nations. We have begun to see how God can bring social change through soul change, in individuals, communities and even nations.

We invite you to join us in this quest to see what God is doing in our day and to join the Holy Spirit in the work of bringing peace with justice to a divided nation and world.

IS THERE STILL
A RACE PROBLEM?

On July 2, 1999, Ricky Byrdsong, former head basketball coach at Northwestern University, was shot and killed in Skokie, Illinois, the quiet suburban community where he lived. Coach Byrdsong was walking home from a playground with two of his children when a young college student, a self-proclaimed white supremacist, fired from his car and fatally shot him. Ricky died in the hospital later that night—victim of a drive-by shooting by a person he didn't even know.

That same weekend the white supremacist wounded several Jewish people in Chicago, fired shots at Asian people in downstate Illinois, and killed a Korean doctoral student, Won Joon Yoon, who was standing in front of his Presbyterian church in Indiana. The shooting spree and the senseless loss of human life that resulted were motivated by racial hatred, ethnocentrism and fear. The murders of Coach Ricky Byrdsong and Won Joon Yoon shook up many Christians, but even more, they disturbed a nation that doesn't want to believe that people of color and ethnic Jews can still be vulnerable to such racial hatred and violence.

THE RACE PROBLEM

Unfortunately, this story could be repeated many times over, because there is still a race problem in America. Since September 11, 2001, suspicion, hostility and violence have increased between people from different racial and religious groups. It is estimated that in the next twenty years white Americans will become a minority in the United States, and most of the nation's population will be Asian and Hispanic. The demographic shift deepens an atmosphere of increasing fear and contempt. People of other races, ethnicities and nationalities are often viewed as threats to mainstream Americans' opportunity and economic security. As a result, government programs such as affirmative action are being repealed, and many people speak out vehemently against allowing any more people—usually people of color—to immigrate to this country. In economically uncertain times and in the face of increased globalization, it is no surprise that hate groups, acts of terrorism and racially motivated violence have increased in our nation and around the world.

The tragic events of September 11 reminded us that we cannot continue pursuing our own national self-interest with indifference to other nations and peoples. We must wake up, discern the signs of the times and recognize that we must relate differently to people who are unlike us. September 11 also taught us that we are not able to control the world or to keep ourselves safe. However hard we may try, our technological skills and military might cannot completely guard us from destructive forces. Although we know this to be true, we continue our desperate efforts to get back in control and feel powerful again. Many people grope for coping mechanisms—some legal, some illegal—in vain attempts to control their world and feel safe. Others are choosing the way of violence and isolation, stockpiling weapons and segregating themselves from other people. All of this is evidence of a spirit of fear that is endemic to our society and can be changed only by the Spirit of God.

Billy Graham, the famous international evangelist, recognizes the challenge. Toward the end of his public ministry, he said, "Racial and ethnic hostility is the foremost social problem facing our world today. From the systematic horror of 'ethnic cleansing' in Bosnia to the random violence ravaging our inner cities, our world seems caught up in a tidal wave of racial and ethnic tension. This hostility threatens the very foundations of modern society."[1]

Unfortunately, the Christian church seems woefully inadequate to rouse itself from apathy in the face of these deep-rooted global and social problems. We have failed to proactively declare and demonstrate the truth and power of the gospel to create unity across cultures, ethnicities and nationalities. There is a tremendous disparity between the vision God has for us and our current social reality, and Christians seem powerless to even begin bridging the gap.

Michael Emerson and Christian Smith help us understand our ineffectiveness in their seminal book *Divided by Faith*.[2] These Christian professors provide an outstanding historical and contemporary analysis of how and why the evangelical church has been racist throughout its history. Their findings reveal that evangelical theology itself is partly to blame for the impotence of most Christians in dealing with racial and ethnic injustice. They discovered that most evangelicals view their faith, conversion and transformation as an individual matter that affects society one life at a time. Unfortunately, this theological individualism has rendered most evangelical Christians completely ill-equipped to deal with major social structures or grapple with corporate and institutional evil.

This blindness to the larger forces and institutional realities affects our ability to even see the racial problem in America. The blindness became painfully clear to Rick when he was driving his son and two other kids home from church recently. The conversation in the car focused on the sermon the pastor had preached calling for racial harmony and justice. One of the European American teenagers piped up: "I don't see what the point of that sermon was. I could see it if our church were located in the inner city. But we don't have a race problem in the suburbs of Chicago. Why was the pastor making such a big deal about it? I don't see how it's relevant."

This teen is not alone in his perceptions. You may feel that way too. Although there is an immense interest in racial reconciliation among many young people today, many others manifest disinterest in and apathy about racial issues. Most whites really believe that we no longer have a race problem in our society. They'd like to think all that got solved with the civil rights legislation of the 1960s. Most whites really believe that the playing field has been leveled and equal opportunity has been made available to everybody. As a result, they think minority people should buck up, pull themselves up by their bootstraps, and quit complaining and whining and "playing the race card" every time they want something.

On the other hand, we have observed that most people of color have no doubt that there is still a very significant race problem in America. Not long ago Willow Creek Community Church in Barrington, Illinois, held a weekend service titled "Bridging the Racial Divide." The service began with stories told by people of color who are Willow Creek members and have experienced discrimination.

An African American executive employee of the church told about how he was followed by a police officer after stopping to fill his car with gas. When he pulled over to ask what the problem was, he was told that being black, he fit the description of someone the police were looking for.

An Asian American woman told about going shopping for a coat at a local department store. She found one she wanted and asked an employee to put it aside while she continued shopping. When she returned to buy the jacket, she was shocked to find a white woman walking out with it. The store manager gave her no apology, and she never got the jacket.

Still another story came from a biracial woman who experienced a painful breakup with her boyfriend because his white family rejected her. They did not want him dating an African American and couldn't stand the idea of having mixed-race grandchildren. The rejection left a deep scar on the young woman's heart. She began to wonder whether she would ever find true acceptance at a predominantly white church.

The last story was a Latino man's recounting of a painful memory from his childhood. He worked as a caddy at a golf course. On his day off he invited a friend to come and swim with him, since this was one of the perks of the job. His friend was ordered out of the pool, and when he asked why he was told, "We don't allow Hispanics in here." Since the caddy had fair skin, they had assumed he himself was Anglo. They said they would make an exception for him, but instead he chose to quit his job that day.

These stories moved and shocked many of the white members of the Willow Creek congregation, who had assumed that those kinds of things just don't happen anymore. But people of color in the congregation were not shocked at all. They know these kinds of things happen all the time.

If you think about it, it makes sense. Blacks live with the residual effects of four hundred years of unthinkable oppression at the hands of white people of northern European origin. Native Americans live with the past experience of an almost totally successful genocide campaign against them, again by whites of northern European background. Latino people experienced conquest by southern Europeans of Spanish background and then lost the whole of the Southwest United States to whites of northern European background. Asian Americans experienced hatred and resentment in the early years of immigration, during World War II after the Pearl Harbor attack when many were put into internment camps, and more recently because their economic and educational success has angered many whites who feel disempowered by the success of other groups. Most people of color are keenly aware of all the continuing interpersonal and systemic inequities in America.

HOW SHOULD WE RESPOND?

What should the church's response be in a world being torn apart by prejudice, hatred and fear? We believe it is imperative that the Christian church regain its integrity to address injustice. This will require that we relinquish the individualism and isolation that have been prevalent among evangelical Christians in the past, so that we can develop new models of racial reconciliation, social justice and spiritual healing. Our unity and reconciliation efforts could be the greatest witness of the church to the power of the gospel in the twenty-first century.

So let's look at the mission of the church in the twenty-first century to bring reconciliation to a divided and wounded world. But first, let's pause and pray.

Each chapter in this book closes with our prayer about the themes of the chapter. Make this prayer your own and pray with us. Racial reconciliation is a spiritual issue, and we are called to prayer that moves us into action.

God, too often our hearts and eyes have been closed to the suffering of others in our racially divided world. Give us eyes to see and hearts that share your heart for the unity and reconciliation of all peoples. We pray in your name. Amen.

2

MISSION IMPOSSIBLE?

Your *mission, should you choose to accept it, is to bridge the dividing walls of hostility that are tearing our world apart.*

We face a mission that seems impossible. The world is becoming increasingly global and multiethnic. We are experiencing more racial and ethnic diversity—and the challenges that come with it—than any generation that has ever preceded us.

In the face of this reality we are called to work together to make this world a better place—to represent the kingdom of God on earth. We are called to more than tolerance or political correctness. We are to be the Reconciliation Generation!

Does this call motivate and stir you? Or does it sound like wishful thinking? In our own strength this mission *is* impossible. The hatred and injustice, the loss of lives to terrorism around the world, the deaths of so many past freedom fighters and champions of justice, the legacy of slavery and of segregation, the racial prejudices and fears that produce tribal wars and ethnic cleansing—it all seems insurmountable. No wonder many people today believe that racial and ethnic reconciliation is just a dream based in unreality. But is it?

GOD IS MOVING

It is vital for God's people to recognize when God is moving significantly in history. A divinely orchestrated major shift in the course of human affairs is called *kairos* time. Kairos time is not determined or controlled by human beings. It is a time frame that is completely controlled by God. *Kairos*—the transliteration of a Greek word for time—signifies the right time, the set time, the opportune time, the strategic time or the decisive time.

This concept is unfamiliar to Western thinking, so it's helpful to make an analogy with pregnancy. A husband and wife conceive a child, then wait for months in anticipation of their child's birth. Although technology makes it possible for parents-in-waiting to know the gender of their child and whether there are potential health problems, there is still much that remains unknown. So the expectant parents eagerly wait, hope and pray. The mother gains weight, her body changes in other ways, she begins to have trouble sleeping. There are signs all along the way that something is happening—that they are progressing toward the birth of the little one they have been waiting for.

And then one day or night, likely at some inconvenient time when the couple least expects it, the woman starts to feel something unusual. She turns to her husband, who is no doubt sound asleep, and nudges him gently but firmly. Then she says in a calm but somewhat urgent voice, "Honey, wake up. It's time!" He knows exactly what that means, so he jumps up and begins to take action.

That's kairos time! It is the fulfillment of what we have been waiting for. The process has been beyond our control, and now it calls us to spring into action. Kairos time always demands a response.

We believe that a kairos moment is upon us. What will our response be? Will you collaborate with God and be part of the generation God uses to establish his multiethnic kingdom on earth?

RAISING UP A GENERATION

We believe that God will use the emerging generation (late teens, twenties and early thirties) to bring about spiritual healing and racial reconciliation. Today's young people have grown up in a multicultural and multiethnic world, and they have a great spiritual hunger. They have seen the results of shattered relationships, family brokenness, racial and ethnic hatred, wars and terrorism. They want a different path—a path of reconciliation, mutual respect and understanding, a path that leads to connection. This longing lies deep within the next generation, and we believe that God will bless their desire.

We believe that this generation will take the torch and make the gains that former generations only dreamed of. They are not comfortable with divisions based on racial and ethnic categories. They don't want to categorize people in ways that divide, segregate and separate them. They are deeply sensitive to issues of trust and authority and are not interested in following people who are merely building their own kingdom or feathering their own nest. This generation will not lead people in ways that use and devalue them. They want more than a role reversal in which the people who want power replace the people who had power. They don't want to play the same game with different winners. Instead these emerging leaders want a new game, a game that is just, a way of life that honors people and relationships in true community.

We all have a part to play, and this book will hopefully help all of us. But the emerging generation has a particularly strategic part to play at this kairos moment in history.

THE SPIRITUAL BATTLE

How will we fight the battle for justice and reconciliation? This battle is personal and institutional, but it is more—it is a spiritual battle. The apostle Paul teaches us that there are spiritual forces and realities all around us. In Ephesians 6 he states clearly that our battle is not against flesh and blood but against rulers, authorities, powers and spiritual forces of evil in the heavenly realms. Our weapons are not the weapons of this world. As Christians, we must use spiritual weapons that have divine power to demolish strongholds of racism, hatred, oppression, injustice and fear.

So we do not depend only on our relational skills and abilities, arm ourselves only with good intentions and insightful social analysis. Social analysis, however brilliant and incisive, may help us understand the problem, but by itself can never solve the problem. Racism and injustice, division and hatred are spiritual problems. They are evil. Ultimately, only one power in the world can solve the problem of evil. Only the power of the cross, only the life and death and resurrection of Jesus of Nazareth, can open the way of life, hope and reconciliation.

But what does that mean? What do these spiritual weapons consist of? How do we employ them in the battle? How are the cross and resurrection and the gift of the Spirit adequate responses to the problem of racial hatred, pride, fear and division? Too often people and institutions that emphasize the spiritual world have ignored poverty, injustice, racism and hatred. How will we use our faith as a force for change and not merely another smokescreen for self-protection and self-interest? How will we pursue spiritual solutions and spiritual weapons in a way that solves and doesn't just reinforce the great problems of our society? The chapters that follow will help you wrestle with each of these questions. We will explore how worship, healing prayer and spiritual warfare can lead to the healing of people and nations. We will see how *soul change* leads to *social change*.

There are no quick fixes. And the journey is costly. However, we challenge you to recognize that we are living in a strategic time in history. God is moving, and something new, exciting and powerful is about to happen in the world! Instead of relying on our own strength and ingenuity, we are called to partner with God in what he is doing.

HEALING PEOPLE AND NATIONS

Mahatma Gandhi, the great Asian Indian leader, rejected Christian faith for two reasons. First, he could not accept the Christian meaning of the death of Jesus. His second reason was that he experienced the powerlessness of Christian faith to bring unity and justice in South Africa and then in his dealings with the British in India. When asked how Christians could better witness to Jesus, he replied, "Live like Jesus did, and the world will listen."[1]

Jesus prayed that we all might be one in his last recorded prayer: "As you, Father, are in me and I am in you, may they also be in us, so that the world may believe that you have sent me" (John 17:21). For Jesus, genuine Christian unity is the supreme sign of the power and truth of the gospel for a watching world. Our failure to live out this reality deeply grieves the heart of God. Scripture tells us that when we grieve the Holy Spirit, the Spirit of God withdraws his blessing and presence. The glory of the Lord departs. How much have the church's witness and impact suffered over the centuries because of racial and ethnic divisions and hatreds?

Scripture also tells us in Exodus 20:5 and Deuteronomy 5:9 that God "visits" sins and their consequences to the third and fourth generation. Unconfessed sin festers in the soul of a nation. Unrepented evil remains in the consciousness of a nation. Unrenounced idolatry has a devastating effect on later generations. Our nation's commitment to economic supremacy has often been an idolatry whose consequences have reverberated down through generations. We are dealing with generational sin and bondage as a nation when it comes to racism, ethnic hatred and violence. Many other nations in which ethnic hatred and violence are pervasive are also struggling within this kind of intergenerational bondage.

God wants to break into that cycle, and God wants his church to take the lead in repentance, renunciation and humility. We believe that a wave of the Spirit is coming, a mighty outpouring of the presence of God. Racial and ethnic reconciliation will be a distinguishing mark, maybe even *the* distinguishing mark, of this next outpouring of God's Spirit. What God is raising up is global in scope and scale and absolutely stunning in impact and importance, given the pressing global struggles we face. As we together repent of sins and renounce the idolatries that have divided us, as we break patterns that have bound us across generations, God will be delighted to bring a great revival to his people and a great advance of his gospel.

The question each of us faces is, will we respond and become part of this work of God's Spirit in our day? Will we collaborate with God and be a part of what he is doing in the earth? To do this we must be willing to face the truth and come out of our denial. We have to see the racism and injustice that exist all around us. We must also see and acknowledge our need for God to empower us in this process of reconciliation if our efforts are to be successful.

We have written this book because we want you to discover how to connect to the immense spiritual resources and power that God wants to pour on his people to heal the soul of our nations. As a black woman and a white man who have been friends and colleagues for over ten years, we have both experienced the pain and disillusionment of working for racial justice. We have a history of working together to promote racial reconciliation in InterVarsity Christian Fellowship. We have cried and prayed with other brothers and sisters in the struggle when the changes we sought were too slow in coming. For years we have observed each other's integrity as we have made hard choices with our spouses to live out racial reconciliation in our personal lives. We have not always been successful; we know firsthand how hard this battle is. But we continue to have hope because we both believe in the prophetic power of the Holy Spirit. We believe that God is active in human affairs. We are convinced, more than ever, that a vital missing aspect of the war on racial injustice is to recognize the truth of what God says in Zechariah 4:6: "Not by might, nor by power, but by my Spirit, says the LORD of hosts."

It is our firm belief and conviction that reconciliation is ultimately a spiritual process. We need a spirituality of racial and ethnic reconciliation that will take us beyond our limitations. In our human strength racial reconciliation is impossible. We are not able to change our hearts and transform our lives without the intervention of God. Without God's presence and power, we are destined to stay locked in destructive patterns of racial and ethnic conflict and division that we can analyze but not change.

So we call on you to ready yourself to engage in the struggle—the great spiritual battle for the soul of our nations and the souls of all people. Racism and injustice are a cancer on the soul of our nation and a sickness in the souls of people. Together we are committed to ministering hope and healing to people of every ethnicity and nationality who long to catch the vision and experience God's powerful ministry of reconciliation among all the nations of the earth. Will you join us on this journey?

Let's pray:

O God, Father of every people on earth and Redeemer of every nation under the sun, pour out your Spirit. Illumine our minds with the truths of your gospel that liberate us from the power of Satan and that reconcile us to our enemies, ancient and contemporary. We need you, Lord, to intervene. On our own we have no hope. But with you, and your Son, and the gift of your Spirit, we believe the time has come for a great awakening in our nation that brings all your children together to stand for your kingdom of justice and love.

God, your kingdom come, your will be done on earth as it is in heaven.

Bring glory to your name in these days. Establish your victory over the sins of our fathers and mothers and over the spirits of evil at work to destroy the people.

Lord, teach us to pray. Help us to preach your kingdom. And teach us to receive and minister your healing power.

We pray in your name. Amen.

A BETTER WAY

In preparing to teach a seminar on the book of Acts together, we discovered some interesting things about ourselves. As we wrestled with Acts 2, Brenda kept pointing out the multiethnic and multicultural dimensions of this text. She said that it was not by accident that God revealed his Spirit and proclaimed the gospel to Jewish converts who were from many nations and spoke many different languages.

Rick, on the other hand, felt that she was making too big an issue of the cultural and ethnic dimensions. He believed the disciples spoke in many tongues because it was necessary for them to communicate the gospel to the different people who had gathered in Jerusalem. In his view, God was just making a strategic evangelistic and communication move. The diversity of language and the diversity of the first community were a means to an end: reaching all the individuals present with the good news about Jesus.

Brenda kept seeing more significance to the makeup of this first church. She emphasized that the gospel is not only a message about saving individuals but also a message about reconciling the nations. Thus, the gospel proclamation was accompanied by a reconciled community—a sign that God was at work. (We have begun to think that a reconciled community may even be the sign of the in-breaking kingdom of God in our day as well.)

Rick realized as he and Brenda worked together on Acts that he had not had eyes to see how crucial the corporate reconciliation themes were in the book of Acts. Rick had been taught to see the text through an individualistic lens and to focus on the salvation of individuals. He had not been taught to look for the corporate and social dimensions of that salvation. Rick had seen those themes in other parts of Scripture, in the Old Testament for instance. But he had not seen those themes as clearly in the book of Acts.

As we continued to work through Acts, we discovered that well intentioned, godly, deeply committed, Spirit-filled Christians could also be ethnocentric and bigoted. We saw that over and over again the disciples fell back into comfortable ethnocentric patterns and that only God's miraculous interventions forced them out of their cultural and religious prejudices and isolation. In many ways the book of Acts is the story of how the Holy Spirit takes ethnocentric people, changes them and calls them to carry the gospel across every ethnic and cultural boundary. It was imperative that these early disciples overcome their ethnocentrism, because reconciliation is at the core of the gospel and is vital for the healing of people and the healing of nations. It is also imperative that we overcome our ethnocentrism that the gospel might move forward in our divided world.

TAKING OFF OUR BLINDERS

The gospel was always intended to transform groups of people and to empower them to confront larger spiritual forces. However, because white Americans' understanding of sin and transformation is highly individualistic, we have often remained powerless and silent before the greatest spirits of the age—spirits of racial superiority and idolatry. Such ignorance of corporate principalities and powers helps to explain how the church in Germany and the Western world remained largely silent in the face of the genocide of Jews. Our ignorance and silence have cost us dearly, calling into question our credibility and the gospel's power to heal and remake our society.

God has always had a great purpose for cultures, nations and peoples. This purpose, which is to fill the earth and bring it under the reign of God, requires that humanity in all its diversity reflect the image of God in the earth. When human beings pursue this "cultural mandate," we participate in the coming of the kingdom of God.

Human beings were made in the image of God—distinct from all other earthly creatures—to be in a self-aware relationship of union and fellowship with God. As an expression of this divine intimacy, the human vocation was to fill the earth and subdue it and to be God's representative or "image" in the world. The book of Genesis gives us the purpose of human beings in the world:

God created humankind in his own image,
in the image of God he created them;
male and female he created them.
God blessed them, and God said to them, "Be fruitful and multiply, and fill the earth and subdue it." (Genesis 1:27-28)

To fulfill this mandate, humans had to multiply and form kinship groups. These emerging kinship groupings, as they spread, created culture in response to many different environments. They developed farming and farming implements, hunting and hunting weapons, food storage facilities and methods, means of communication, marriage rituals and worship practices.[1] This is why theologians call the Genesis command to be fruitful, multiply, fill the earth and subdue or steward it the *cultural mandate*.

Many Christians have not understood or embraced this global cultural mandate. Conservative Protestant Christians have instead emphasized the Great Commission—the call to preach the gospel to the ends of the earth. Other Christians, who may be characterized as more liberal, have placed emphasis on the Great Commandment—the imperative to love our neighbors as ourselves and to see all people as our fellow citizens. Although both the Great Commandment and the Great Commission are central to our faith, they presuppose the global cultural mandate that commands us to fill the earth as God's representatives and stewards.

To fulfill God's command, human beings had to become creators of kinship networks, diverse cultures and ultimately many nations. As human beings spread and diversified, racial differences also emerged. These racial differences were a part of God's intention from the beginning. They were intended to be a part of the beauty and variety of the image of God on the earth. Although God invites humanity to do the work, race, culture and ethnicity began in God's heart, mind and intention. God has always had a great purpose for our ethnic and cultural diversity. He did not "suggest" the cultural enterprise—he commanded it! However, human beings and the unseen powers that influence human behavior had other plans.

The story of the Tower of Babel in Genesis 11 tells of a people group who refused to spread and fill the earth. Instead they defiantly sought to hold on to their homogeneity and their centralized form of government. As a reflection of their defiance, arrogance and self-reliance, they decided to build a tower that would express their pride and autonomy from God. In so doing, they would stop the fulfillment of the God's global cultural command.

In response to this rebellion and attempted self-protection, God intervened, confused their languages and scattered the people. As a result, God's intended purpose for the spread and diversification of humanity and cultures would continue.

Babel is the story of every fallen human people and nation. In every case the technological, military, commercial or political achievements of a nation become the basis for pride, autonomy and disobedience to God. The precise shape of self-worship changes for each nation, but the ultimate purpose of idolatry—as it was for Babel—is to make a name for ourselves. *Ethnocentrism* is the belief that one's people group is superior, more vital and significant than others. It reflects our efforts to feel powerful and defended. The Tower of Babel is an indication of how we use social grouping and technology to defend ourselves against God—God's mandate, God's power and God's threat—because it is God who would make us disperse.

This propensity to defend ourselves against God is evident in how European Americans made the gospel ethnocentric. In recent centuries missionaries took the gospel to Africa, Asia and other parts of the world but wove cultural compliance into their evangelical fervor. The message was that to become a Christian was to *be like us*—to be assimilated culturally. For all intents and purposes, Christ looks like us. If a culture does not look like us, then it is un-Christlike. In essence, what European Americans did—although this is not limited to white people, because we all have the tendency to be ethnocentric—was to say that if you want to be a Christian like me, you will have to adopt my cultural position and lose your own.

Such a devaluing of cultural distinctions comes from a tendency to assume that there is an "ultimate" and that the ultimate is us. Like the people at the Tower of Babel, American Christians have attempted to build a global monument to ourselves. We have owned Christianity to such an extent that we cannot differentiate between what is Christian and what is our culture. We have wrapped them up together—flag, Bible, country—so that the ultimate form of Christianity looks like us. That is the epitome of ethnocentrism, and it wipes out all other cultural distinctions.

This is not Christianity. It is what Carl Ellis calls "Christianity-ism" in his very insightful book *Beyond Liberation*. God is not the author of "Christianity-ism." This is a cultural construct that has robbed the true gospel of its relevance and its power. God deals with cultural distinctions in a radically different way, which is demonstrated for us in Acts 2.

BREAKING FREE

On the day of Pentecost in Jerusalem, the Holy Spirit—God's invisible, powerful presence—came to empower the disciples to fulfill his global cultural mandate. They had been called to be witnesses of Jesus Christ "to the ends of the earth" (Acts 1:8), but their ethnocentrism was one of the main barriers to the spread of the gospel beyond the Jewish people. At Pentecost, then, God intervenes and does something absolutely amazing—he allows people to hear the gospel in their mother tongue!

The diversity of languages at Pentecost suggests something about the diversity of God's movement in the earth. Instead of hostility between these people groups, somehow the Spirit's recognition and affirmation of their diverse ethnic identities creates intimacy. It creates a sense that God cares about them; God loves them and knows who they are intimately. The message of Pentecost is *you are important to God*. Your distinctiveness is valued—God knows you so well that he speaks your language! This is true intimacy, and the foreigners gathered in Jerusalem were stunned that God would choose intimacy with them.

People appreciate it when we try to speak their language. In the summer of 1998 Brenda's husband, Derek, had the privilege of visiting South Africa and Zimbabwe. In Zimbabwe he met an older man who became confused because Derek looked African but could not speak the Ndebele language. When Derek finally mustered a few words in this man's native language, he was rewarded with a smile of great pleasure and pride. Now he could identify with Derek in a new way. This foreigner had somehow become familiar to him—a part of the human race that he could embrace. A bonding across nationalities and cultures occurred because one man tried to engage another man on a level that was intimate and personal.

This is exactly what happened on the day of Pentecost. People from all over the known world could say, "God speaks my language! God knows my identity. God knows who I am." In other words, my ethnic identity is recognized and valued by God.

This security allows us to go out into a world that is being fragmented by nationalism, racism, sexism, ethnocentrism, individualism and materialism and proclaim that there is a better way. As representatives of the kingdom of God made up of people from every tribe, ethnic group and nationality we are called to demonstrate the power of the gospel to reconcile diverse people into one new humanity. However, like the disciples in the book of Acts, we must not make our ethnic identity the most salient or central part of who we are.

Christ says to us, "I want to be your most important identity." Christ is more important than our racial or ethnic identities. This does not cancel or dismiss our cultural identity; it simply supersedes them as the most significant. That's why Jesus says in Matthew 10:34-36 that he came to fulfill the prophecy of Micah 7:6: "For a son treats his father with contempt, the daughter rises up against her mother, the daughter-in-law against her mother-in-law; your enemies are members of your own household." In other words, our identity with Christ becomes more important than our family, heritage, culture or ethnic identity. Jesus goes on to say in Matthew 10:37-39, "Whoever loves father or mother more than me is not worthy of me; and whoever loves son or daughter more than me is not worthy of me. . . . Those who find their life will lose it, and those who lose their life for my sake will find it." The message of Jesus is clear. Anyone who identifies more with their family, their culture or their ethnic heritage is not worthy of Christ. Willingness to relinquish these other identities as most important is the path the leads to true and lasting life.

Jesus Christ asks us to surrender absolutely everything, but in so doing he does not wipe out our ethnic identity. He forces us to affirm that our identity with him is the most salient. This is echoed by the apostle

Paul in Galatians 3:28: "There is no longer Jew nor Greek, there is no longer slave or free, there is no longer male and female; for all of you are one in Christ Jesus." Unfortunately, some people have wrongly interpreted this text to mean that culture and gender are irrelevant to our ultimate identity and relationships in the kingdom of God. We believe that in the kingdom there is no longer Jew or Greek, male or female, or any other dividing distinctions—but not because those aspects of our personhood are erased. Instead they are deepened and transcended. We become more than male and female, more than our ethnicity, culture or nationality—never less. The future vision of the kingdom is the fulfillment of our race, culture and gender, not their erasure.

Throughout scripture we can see that God handles our cultural and ethnic distinctiveness quite differently from the way we do. We tend to build empires to ourselves as opposed to building the kingdom of God. An empire conquers peoples to make them all subject to one ruler. God's kingdom draws all peoples based on an intimate knowledge of who they are. God's ultimate call to each of us is, "Become a part of my family and me because I know you—I know you intimately." We must not value our human or ethnic identity as the end goal. Instead, we must understand that the end is—and must always be—the relationship with God and God's family in God's kingdom.

God has always had a great purpose for cultures, nations and peoples. We are called to fill the earth and bring it under the reign of God. This will require that humanity in all its diversity reflect the image of God. This is our mission as ambassadors of the kingdom of God. We are called to pursue the kingdom as our highest priority. This suggests that God wants our main identity to be rooted in our relationship with him. Our identity with God and our allegiance to him require that we pursue the things that are important to him. Again, this does not wipe out our ethnic identity, but it changes the structuring of our priorities and the way we relate to people.

Putting the kingdom first means that we must relate to Christians differently from the way we relate to our own people group. The people of our racial, ethnic or cultural group are no longer our most significant point of identity. Instead, our identity is rooted in our connection to Christ and his people. They become our new extended family. This is the reality that the apostle Paul affirms in Ephesians 2:14-16:

> He is our peace; in his flesh he has made both groups into one and has broken down the dividing wall, that is, the hostility between us. He has abolished the law with its commandments and ordinances, that he might create in himself one new humanity in place of the two, thus making peace, and might reconcile both groups to God in one body through the cross, thus putting to death that hostility through it.

Our God is a God of reconciliation. Ethnocentrism and racism always carry with them an understanding of salvation that violates the truth of the gospel and the necessity of the cross. Whenever our community reinforces splitting the new humanity back into its separate and alienated parts, the gospel has been undone.

This new reality of unity in diversity, this new act of creation, is the better way God offers to us. From the very beginning God has cared about all the nations of the earth. It is vital that we reclaim this important understanding of Scripture and allow our ethnic identity to be healed so that we can actively participate in the coming of the kingdom. Our ethnicity is a part of what God will use to reconcile all things under Christ. Ethnic identity and reconciliation with other people are central to being a citizen of the kingdom of God.

As ambassadors of this kingdom, we need to understand that the ethnic element of our identity will not just disappear when Christ returns. Revelation 7:9 gives us a glimpse into the future, when the kingdom of God will be made up of "a great multitude that no one could count, from all tribes and peoples and languages." Here in the kingdom the human hunger for all people to be one will be ultimately satisfied. Yet in that oneness, every tribe and tongue and people and nation will be recognizable. What is distinctive about us will not just disappear. We will see clearly the human diversity and beauty.

And not only are all tribes and tongues and peoples and nations visible, but the cultural products of these groups are also present at the consummation of the kingdom. The scene of multiethnic unity is picked up again in Revelation 21—22, where we are told that the kings of the nations come into the New Jerusalem bearing the glories of their nations to lay at the feet of the Lamb, Jesus the Christ. The glory of the nations, the unique giftedness and goodness of each culture, will be there at the end and will last forever.[2]

SPREADING THE WORD

As we shared this message during one seminar, students began to catch the vision and embrace this new reality. At the end of the seminar a young white woman named Jenny stood in a large group of students and said to us all, "I was blown away by this conference! First I realized that God cares a lot about ethnicity and culture. He made us as human beings to be culture creators and to spread across the earth and diversify. I always thought my ethnic and cultural identity was a part of me that was secondary and unimportant to God. But it really matters to God! He has a purpose for that part of who we are. I always thought of myself as 'white generic American' and didn't really accept that part of who I am. Honestly, I just felt guilty about being white. It was so powerful for me to start to recognize my ethnic identity (yes, 'white generic American' is a valid ethnic background!) and see it as a gift from God to embrace and explore and celebrate. Finally, I realize that I need to speak up whenever people around me insult or slight the ethnic and racial backgrounds of others. I can make a difference!"

Jenny got it! She began to see Scripture with new eyes, and it was changing the way she saw herself and others and giving her resources to reconcile with others and to fight the battle for justice. We will never be fully used to help bring about the healing of people and of nations until we understand that God's purpose and plan includes our racial and ethnic identity.

God, thank you that you made us in your image to fill the earth and to bring all things under your reign. Thank you that you have called us to be culture creators and have given us our ethnic backgrounds as a gift. We confess that we have misused this gift and rebelled against you through our ethnocentrism and pride. We ask your forgiveness for our part, by ignorance, silence or active participation, in excluding and judging other people. Thank you that you have given all peoples, as beings made in your image, the capacity to participate in your kingdom. Praise you, Lord, that my ethnic identity is a part of your good purpose and plan for my life and for the world. We look forward to the day when people from every tribe, tongue, people and nation will worship you together with all that we have and all that we are in the kingdom of God. Amen.

4

A NEW MODEL

Developing a strong interracial friendship has been a difficult and challenging journey for us. Our personal failures over the years and our experiences of immense pain in this battle for racial reconciliation and justice sometimes caused us to misunderstand and even mistrust each other's motives and intentions. We realized that we were both engaged in an intense war for racial and ethnic reconciliation, but we hadn't understood the stress it would place on our friendship.

Looking back, we can see that there have been many casualties of war on this particular battlefront. In fact, in one year Rick experienced so much loss and pain as he watched people that he knew and loved die, burn out or drop out of the battle for reconciliation that he almost became a casualty of war himself.

In the late 1980s Rick was the area director for InterVarsity Christian Fellowship in Chicago. Rick has always longed for racial reconciliation to be a core value in his life and ministry. So he used his position and influence as area director to spearhead a major initiative for racial reconciliation and justice on college campuses in the Chicago area. He partnered with other Christian leaders—a Latino, an Asian Indian and an African American—and they committed themselves together to pursuing interpersonal relationships across ethnic and racial lines. They started a minority student retention program together and raised a lot of money to fund it.

Then a series of tragedies hit. The African American leader, who had national responsibility for InterVarsity's Black Campus Ministry, went through a painful and very confusing divorce, which resulted in his withdrawing from the leadership of the program. Rick began experiencing what seemed like irresolvable tensions in his relationships with the black staff who remained on the InterVarsity team.

In the same month that they found out about the divorce, the Latino team leader arrived at Rick's home for a staff meeting. Shortly after arriving, he suffered a massive heart attack and died in Rick's living room.

Meanwhile, Rick was also facing tensions at home because of his frequent absences as he tried to stem the oncoming tide of failure. Although he worked long and hard hours trying to build a crosscultural ministry, the interpersonal conflicts on the team just seemed to be multiplying. Rick ended up feeling rejected and blamed by some of the ethnic people of color he had hoped to serve. He also faced the possible loss of his job because of the financial losses the project suffered. It was the most serious professional and personal crisis of Rick's life.

Rick had already invited Brenda to join his staff, and she arrived just as the program was beginning to fold. Rick and others spent the next year picking up the pieces, but Brenda was unaware of the huge sacrifice he had made and the great losses he had suffered. After hiring her, he moved on to a new job, found a new ministry focus and moved out of the city. Brenda couldn't help but see him as just another white person who talked a good game but left the battle when things got too tough and retreated to the safety of the suburbs.

The turning point came several years later, when Brenda decided to go get Rick and invite him back into the fray. We met at a Bennigan's restaurant, and we will never forget the conversation that ensued. Brenda began to probe and ask questions. Rick's answers helped her to better understand the immensity of the hurt he felt over his failure and the death of his dream. Rick had blocked off many of the memories and hadn't realized that he had repressed some very deep feelings. For her part, Brenda told Rick about many experiences with white people who had used her and other black people to help assuage their guilt, only to leave when it was no longer convenient or comfortable for them to be involved.

As we continued to talk and share, healing began to take place at that meal. After our conversation was over, a former casualty of war was restored and recommissioned for the battle, and a deeper friendship was forged between us.

As we began to dream again, we were and are painfully aware of how many other casualties this war has claimed. Death, divorce, fatigue, burnout and broken relationships have all seemed to plague leaders of racial reconciliation ministries. We will never forget the death of our dear brother Spencer Perkins, who cohosted a powerful conference on racial reconciliation with Chris Rice, his friend and long-term partner in ministry. This life-changing conference was the first of its kind and was attended by hundreds of people committed to racial reconciliation from all over the United States. Spencer collapsed at that conference, recovered and delivered a dynamic message on the need for grace in racial reconciliation. But shortly after the conference, he died in his home.

Just two years later Alex Anderson, another dear friend, mentor and pioneer in black campus ministry and racial reconciliation for InterVarsity Christian Fellowship, died of a massive heart attack in his mid-forties. We could cite many more examples of the extreme price people have paid in the battle for racial healing and justice.

In an e-mail after Spencer's death, Chris Rice wrote, "I have no clue what is going on these days but it feels as if a war is being waged between good and evil in the heavenlies and somehow it is affecting us down here. The attack on our leaders seems to be getting more and more serious." Why has there been so much pain, so many untimely deaths, so many broken and fractured relationships? Why has so much expenditure of money, effort, time and energy brought so little progress and change? What is the need of the hour that would lead us to be more effective in a worldwide ministry of ethnic and racial reconciliation? We believe that what is needed in this hour is a change strategy that goes beyond the present models we currently pursue.

PRESENT MODELS

Two primary models have been used by great people of faith in America to overcome the racial divisions and inequities of our society. The first is what we refer to as the *relational or interpersonal model*. It can be summarized this way: Make a friend with someone from another race or ethnicity, and you will bring about social change through friendship, one life at a time. This model seeks to address the isolation and ignorance that feed racism and injustice by encouraging interracial friendships that will dismantle inequality and discrimination over time.

This relational model has several strengths. First of all, it is feasible. You don't have to be an expert in racial and ethnic reconciliation to do it. Such simplicity can be extremely motivating for people who are newly interested in the ministry of reconciliation and need a realistic way to get started. The relational model also fits the basic worldview of many evangelical Christians, who understand the gospel in individual and interpersonal terms.

But it is not an adequate change strategy, because it has nothing to say about the historical impact of sin and evil and the way this history has led to structural injustice that cannot be changed by the "one life at a time" approach. In addition, the friendship model does not bring adequate spiritual resources to bear on the immense problems of injustice, rage, guilt, shame and deep woundedness. The depth of pain and hurt go far beyond what most relationships can absorb. Without profoundly spiritual and even miraculous intervention and healing, many cross-ethnic interpersonal relationships are doomed to a constant cycle of frustration, misunderstanding and further wounding. Developing a personal friendship with someone of another ethnicity is still probably the most important first step we can take, but it's not an adequate change model to address the immense challenges we face.

The second paradigm is what we call the *institutional change model*. This method seeks to create justice and equity by redistributing power among groups. Advocates of this approach would support hiring more people of color within an organization, mobilizing people to vote, using economic power through boycotts, job training, community organizing, public school reform and the like. There are definite strengths to this proactive model. First of all, it encourages people to take responsibility for their own destiny. It empowers them with knowledge and skills to make new choices for their future. It is also realistic and takes into account the sociopolitical history that often works against reconciliation, justice and equity.

The problem with this model, however, is that it reduces all relationships to relations of power. The kingdom of God is about more than group competition for power. The biblical ethic of love can never characterize human relationships that are built solely on competition for power. The answer is not merely to reverse the roles and rules of the game. The goal is not merely to give the poor, oppressed and wounded the upper hand. We need new rules and roles, and a new partnership that is not focused on who is the top dog and who is the underdog. Our goal is to be transformed toward God's multiethnic kingdom of worship and *shalom,* which is the Hebrew word for God's peace with justice. The institutional change model is inadequate to accomplish that because it does not address the transformation of the human heart.

In the face of these limitations in our present models, we have been seeking a new approach and have turned to the ministry of healing. We have adapted and applied biblical, pastoral, spiritual and psychological insights from the ministry of healing to problems of racial and ethnic division and hurt. For relationships to change, hearts must change. Here's how Oscar Romero, the late archbishop of El Salvador, and an outstanding spiritual leader and advocate for peace and social justice, describes the need for change to begin with the human heart:

> How easy it is to denounce structural injustice, institutionalized violence, social sin! And it is true, this sin is everywhere, but where are the roots of this social sin? In the heart of every human being. Present day society is a sort of anonymous world in which no one is willing to admit guilt, and everyone is responsible. We are all sinners, and we have contributed to this massive crime and violence in our country. Salvation begins with the human person, with human dignity, with saving every person from sin. And in Lent this is God's call: Be converted![1]

That is why the model we propose focuses on changing hearts and transforming lives—first of individual people and then of whole communities.

HEALING MODEL

In the past the healing ministry has been effectively applied to issues of personal identity, sexual brokenness, gender confusion and relational healing,[2] but not to ethnic identity and cross-ethnic reconciliation. Another limitation has been that the healing model has primarily been individualistic and not sufficiently adapted to corporate issues such as interpersonal or social conflict and hostility.

Since we both have a deep respect for the charismatic and Pentecostal spiritual traditions and believe that they offer great insights into the practice of corporate healing, we have developed a healing ministry model for ethnic and racial reconciliation. We long to see individuals reconciled cross-ethnically and to see whole communities reconciled to partner together in new ways, with a new level of trust based on God's presence to heal and empower people to minister in a broken world. We long to see a generation of leaders responding to the call to the ministry of healing people and nations for the glory of God and for the witness of the church in the world. That is a story worth living for, and that is exactly what this generation needs.

Most of us don't even believe that a world where people of different races, ethnicities and nationalities live together in peace is possible. That's because we've never seen it! Regrettably, there are far too few successful models to refer or relate to. As a result some have lost hope that racial reconciliation is even possible and have opted to settle for tolerance and political correctness. One young woman, Sarah Hinlicky, summed up her feelings about this in an article:

> We can't even imagine a world of cultural or national unity; our world is more like a tattered patchwork quilt. We have every little inconsequential thing, Nintendo 64s and homepages and cell phones, but not one important thing to believe in. What do you have left to persuade us? One thing: the story. We are story people. We know narratives, not ideas. Our surrogate parents were the TV and the VCR, and we can spew out entertainment trivia at the drop of a hat. . . . You wonder why we're so self-destructive, but we're looking for the one story with staying power, the destruction and redemption of our own lives. That's to your advantage: you [Christians] have the best redemption story on the market.[3]

This new story begins and ends with God and offers people of all races and ethnic backgrounds a plot worth living. We are proposing

51

a new healing model of racial and ethnic reconciliation that is rooted in God's story. Present models of racial reconciliation have been very helpful, but we believe they are inadequate to address the urgent need in this generation for a spirituality and community experience that transforms lives. Understanding that racism and ethnic strife are ultimately spiritual problems that demand spiritual solutions, we want to offer an alternative model, not as a replacement but as a complement to the present models, so that we can minister more effectively to the emerging culture.

PRINCIPLES FOR A NEW PARADIGM

We have great respect for the models and the pioneers of racial and ethnic reconciliation who blazed the trail toward justice and reconciliation. Yet because we are convinced that racism and injustice are spiritual problems above all, we offer the healing model of ethnic reconciliation, based on five biblical truths.

First, reconciliation is above all the work of God and happens best in the presence and power of God. Too often we try to engineer reconciliation with human efforts and ignore how utterly overwhelming and impossible reconciliation really is in our broken world. When you consider the slave trade, the Holocaust, genocide in Rwanda, apartheid in South Africa, the marginalization of Palestinians in the Middle East, the near destruction of First Nations people in North America and so many other horrors in history, it makes you wonder how reconciliation between perpetrators and victims can ever occur. In merely human terms, it is impossible.

That's why we need to come into the presence of God to be reminded that with God all things are possible and that God's just and peaceful rule is not merely a pipedream. The dream of the kingdom begins to be realized in the here and now whenever God has been invited and is truly, discernibly present.

Second, reconciliation with others is based on having a healthy sense of one's own identity. When we relate out of woundedness, self-hatred, resentment, rage, self-protectiveness, judgment and fear, relationships will always be distorted and eventually destroyed. Relational healing always involves personal healing, and this requires a healing of our very identity.

At this point we run into some major barriers. Many people of color, at least in the West, need immense healing in order to come into a healthy sense of identity. The negative messages that constantly bombard people of color are pervasive and are extremely damaging to self-esteem. On the other hand, many people in the dominant culture have almost no awareness of their own ethnic identity. They haven't needed to know their ethnic identity in order to experience its benefits. As we seek healing, we can face intense ethnic self-hatred on the one hand and complete ethnic ignorance on the other. Yet to be reconciled we need to know who we are, which includes who we are in our ethnic dimension.

Third, reconciliation is above all rooted in the work of Christ on the cross. At the cross, God suffered for the sake of his enemy—hostile humanity. Through his death on the cross Jesus made it absolutely clear that the offer of forgiveness has been irrevocably given to all humanity. He emphasized this when he prayed for his executioners, "Father, forgive them, for they do not know what they do." At the cross there is forgiveness, healing and freedom for all—perpetrators and victims, sinners and sinned against.

People who have been sinned against in any conflict find the grace to forgive by experiencing the grace of being known intimately and forgiven completely themselves. Robert Schreiter, the author of two seminal books on the spirituality of reconciliation, says, "The victim asks not 'How can I bring myself, as victim, to forgive those who have violated me and my society,' but 'How can I discover the mercy of God welling up in my own life, and where does that lead me?'"[4]

In the process of reconciling a conflict, victims often experience a sense of grace and closure as they tell their stories. Forgiveness without a full disclosure of truth is superficial. Archbishop Desmond Tutu led the Truth and Reconciliation Commission that was established by the South African Parliament on October 21, 1994. This commission aimed at reconciliation rather than revenge and implemented a stunningly powerful model of reconciliation. A key to the model's success was the commitment of Bishop Tutu and the other members of the commission to tell and hear the unvarnished truth in order to bring about true reconciliation and justice. In his book *No Future Without Forgiveness* Bishop Tutu tells many stories of deeply wounded people who found immense healing by just telling their stories and being heard. The Truth and Reconciliation Commission underscored the inseparable link between telling the truth and experiencing reconciliation.

The commission also demonstrated that there is grace for perpetrators of abuse and for the people who have misused power in relationships. When people who have dominated others and used violence to wound hear and identify with the stories of those they have hurt, they are confronted with a new possibility for their humanity. As the perpetrator hears, repents, seeks forgiveness and makes restitution, the reconciliation process comes full circle. As theologian

Miroslav Volf says, "Through God's self-donation, the oppressors, the perpetrators and their sin and violence are atoned for, including them in the communion of God's love. We too must practice self-giving love toward the enemy with the goal of embrace."[5]

Forgiveness is never easy. There are risks: the victim could remain locked in rage, while the dominant person could remain locked in ignorance and apathy, unmoved in the face of suffering. Yet because of the cross, both can be free of the chains of bitterness, rage or unhealthy dominance that bind them. The perpetrator can repent and be free, whether or not the victim ever forgives. The victim can gain freedom by extending forgiveness, whether or not it is ever received and appropriated. Forgiveness is freedom for both victim and perpetrator.

Some people vow to wait for justice before they will entertain the possibility of reconciliation. But seeking an eye for an eye is doomed to frustration and failure. An eye for an eye will lead to a world gone blind. Justice is a wonderful goal and must be our ultimate aim in all relationships, but complete justice can never be realized until God's glory covers the earth. On this side of the return of Christ, justice will always be incomplete and partial. We mere mortals will always judge what is just from our limited and often self-serving perspective. That is why reconciliation must be based on the disclosure of truth and the practice of forgiveness. Only as we are reconciled will we have even the possibility of seeing justice from the other person's point of view. Thus truth telling and forgiveness lie at the heart of the healing model of ethnic reconciliation. They are the crucial steps that make justice a possibility.

Fourth, as we experience forgiveness and the possibility of a new future together, we will realize that there have been larger, destructive forces at work in our common life. The Bible calls these larger forces "principalities and powers" and gives us clear direction on how we should relate to them. We are to relate as free people who worship God and not these idols. We are not to be controlled; rather we are to be discerning and free. We are to renounce the influence and control of these forces in our own lives.

This step of gaining freedom from idols is a crucial but often missing component of contemporary efforts for reconciliation and justice. We need not only repentance and forgiveness of sins but also renunciation of and victory over principalities and powers. Deliverance from the rule of death and demons is an important part of our healing into life and freedom.

The fifth and final step is to individually and corporately embrace being a new creation. Schreiter, a Catholic priest and author of *The Spirituality of Reconciliation,* says, "Reconciliation makes of both victim and oppressor a new creation."[6] As we become a new creation together—individually and corporately—we partner together for reconciliation and justice in the world.

STEPS TOWARD RECONCILIATION

With these principles as the foundation, our model offers specific steps for racial and ethnic reconciliation. The following steps emerge out of the biblical perspectives we have just discussed and form the basis of the spiritual transformation model of ethnic healing and racial justice.

1. *Worship.* We worship God—Father, Son and Holy Spirit—and practice his presence.[7] In so doing, we encounter God's presence and power to melt our hearts and create a new possibility for being

healed, reconciled and re-created as agents together in the global ministry of reconciliation.

2. *Affirming our true ethnic identity and renouncing false identities.* We understand biblically and embrace personally our God-intended ethnic identities. We also learn to identify and renounce distorted and destructive ethnic identities as the idolatries they are. As we embrace a healthy identity, we are empowered to speak the truth with the goal of hearing, healing and being healed.

3. *Receiving and extending forgiveness.* We are all sinners and sinned against, and desperately need forgiveness. So together in God's presence we revisit the personal and corporate memories of our sin and of being sinned against. Bringing our collective and personal memories into the presence of Christ then leads us to acts of extending and receiving forgiveness. These are not superficial actions of excusing and dismissing but genuine, sometimes painful acts of repentance, naming evil for what it is and dealing with it honestly at the cross. In addition, when possible and appropriate, forgiveness will lead to acts of restitution.

4. *Renouncing idols.* Next we name, unmask and renounce the false gods related to racism and ethnocentrism. We renounce the larger spiritual forces of evil that our mothers and fathers and ethnic groups have followed and too often worshiped and obeyed. These forces and past idolatries have controlled and bound us. But just as the cross of Christ brings forgiveness of sin, it also brings freedom from the principalities and powers.

5. *Ongoing partnership.* We are now a new creation, sinner and sinned against, able to embrace and live in the power of the resurrection

and the gift of the Spirit. Together we become agents of reconciliation in a divided world. We will be drawn to those places in the world, like our inner cities and our troubled ethnic hotspots, especially in need of reconciliation modeled and ministered as a witness to the good news and the power of God. But our ongoing partnerships will not just affect ministry in inner cities and in troubled areas of the world. Churches in segregated suburbs will look very different too. Leadership will become more multiethnic, and partnership relationships between diverse churches will become more common.

We are convinced that God is at work in our day to bring healing to a troubled and divided world. As we draw on the resources of Almighty God for healing and restoration, we will no longer be fighting the battle in our own strength.

Dear God, make us new. Bring your Spirit and your joy into all our partnerships with one another so that we will no longer limp along in our relationships, as prisoners to our past. We confess that we are a new creation, victim and perpetrator, sinner and sinned against, filled by the Holy Spirit for the remaking of the world into your kingdom. That kingdom will be built in the end by your power, but bring us into collaboration with you. We want to taste and see that the Lord is good and that his multiethnic kingdom of justice and love has been inaugurated!

HOW WORSHIP
BUILDS BRIDGES

Rick led a concert of prayer at Moody Memorial Church, a large evangelical church that was founded by the famous nineteenth-century evangelist D. L. Moody, in downtown Chicago. The group that met for prayer represented eleven different denominations, including Lutheran, Methodist, Episcopalian, Baptist and Pentecostal. The more than twelve hundred people who gathered for prayer were black, white, Latino, Native American, Asian and international. This diverse group of people held two things in common: a commitment to the lordship of Christ and a dedication to reach the city with the gospel.

The worship began with prayers given in Spanish, Yoruba, Korean and English. The group celebrated to the beat of salsa music and sang contemporary choruses. When a gospel choir led the worship, it felt as if the whole congregation would rise through the roof with praise because God was so powerfully present. These people experienced a unity with one another that honored their different ethnicities and races in a way that is rare in our world. They were being knit together by the Holy Spirit in worship.

In order to prevent divisions and misunderstandings from occurring, it was made perfectly clear that worshipers would focus on the things they held in common and not on controversial doctrinal issues. To promote the spirit of unity, one Latino brother agreed not to speak aloud in tongues, though this was an extremely important part of his prayer life as a Pentecostal believer. Although he kept his word, it became apparent that he had interpreted it loosely. Almost halfway through the worship service he broke out *singing* in tongues!

Rick worried that the rest of the prayer service might go up in flames: he was quite aware that singing in tongues in Moody Memorial Church was *not* the best way to win friends and influence people! So after the concert of prayer Rick went to the senior pastor to apologize. To his surprise and amazement, the pastor shook his hand vigorously and exclaimed how wonderful it was that God had poured out his presence on them. He went on to say that he especially liked the part where the Hispanic brother led the worship in Spanish!

The Latino's singing certainly hadn't sounded like Spanish to Rick. But maybe God translated unknown tongues into Spanish for the senior pastor, or Spanish into tongues for Rick. Who knows? One thing was clear: God had protected the unity of the group that night.

TRANSFORMATION THROUGH WORSHIP

God is delighted when his people come together in worship and prayer to live out the power of the cross to break down dividing walls of hostility. Far too often, those who seek to be reconcilers and peace-makers have anemic worship lives—both individually and corporately. This is a mistake. Racial and ethnic problems are too immense to be addressed with spiritual anemia and cynicism. Rage, mistrust and even self-hatred can lurk in the corners of any heart and cannot be overcome simply by our effort. It takes the Holy Spirit to melt down the inner barriers we have erected and to create in us a desire for God and for other people. This is not humanly manufactured. We can't do it by ourselves. It takes a work of God's grace in our lives.

Writer Anne Lamott discovered this truth and experienced this grace. In her book *Traveling Mercies: Some Thoughts on Faith,* she beautifully describes the spiritual transformation that occurred in her life through worship. Recalling her conversion, she reflects on how she began to attend the worship services of a small, impoverished black church in Marin City, California, St. Andrews Presbyterian:

> But it was the singing that pulled me in and split me open. I could sing better here than I ever had before. As part of these people, even though I stayed in the doorway, I did not recognize my voice or know where it was coming from, but sometimes I felt like I could sing forever.
>
> Eventually, a few months after I started coming, I took a seat in one of the folding chairs, off by myself. Then the singing enveloped me. It was furry and resonant, coming from everyone's very heart. There was no sense of performance or judgment, only that the music was breath and food.
>
> Something inside me that was stiff and rotting would feel soft and tender. Somehow the singing wore down all the boundaries and distinctions that kept me so isolated. Sitting there, standing

with them to sing, sometimes so shaky and sick that I felt like I might tip over, I felt bigger than myself, like I was being taken care of, tricked into coming back to life.[1]

Such softening of our hearts so that the barriers we have erected are broken down and bridges are built between isolated people reveals the miraculous power of worship. When we focus our attention and affection on the God of all creation—the One who made all ethnic groups, tribes and nations and who pours out his presence wherever people are gathered together in his name—all the boundaries and distinctions that keep us separated from each other are worn down, and authentic community and reconciliation result.

Worship is the power that opens us up to the possibility of reconciliation. It fosters an atmosphere of openness, vulnerability and humility that awakens us to what theologian Walter Brueggemann calls the "prophetic imagination." In worship we develop a vision of how God intends the world to be. Brueggemann suggests that Christians are to be a prophetic community whose task is to "nurture, nourish, and evoke a consciousness and perception alternative to the consciousness and perception of the dominant culture around us."[2] It is in worship that this alternative consciousness is developed.

The apostle Paul understood this and therefore urges us in Romans 12:1-2 to offer our bodies as "living sacrifices, holy and pleasing to God—this is your spiritual act of worship" (NIV). According to Paul, worship is more than an event; it is a lifestyle of submission and self-sacrifice motivated by a desire to please God. Paul had an integrated worldview, with no false dichotomies between worship, spirituality and social reality. He calls us to a lifestyle of worship so that we will no longer "conform . . . to the pattern of this world, but be transformed by the renewing of [our] mind" (NIV).

This process of renewal and transformation takes place in worship and prepares us to be prophets who criticize the world's status quo, and it energizes the imagination for what is possible through God. This is what the prophet Isaiah experienced (Isaiah 6). Isaiah was in worship with other priests at the time of this dramatic and life-changing vision. As a priest, he had no doubt been in worship services similar to this one many times before. However, this time something was significantly different. Perhaps he was more open to God or had prepared himself differently to meet with God. It is not clear what predisposed him to be more open, intimate and vulnerable to God this time. The text declares that Isaiah saw God high and exalted, and God's presence enveloped the temple. Isaiah also saw and heard angels—the shining beings that attend the throne of God—worshiping in antiphonal praise, calling to one another, "Holy, holy, holy is the LORD of hosts; the whole earth is full of his glory." As a result of this affirmation and celebration of God's awesome splendor, the presence of God was magnified, and there was a physical manifestation of the Holy Spirit: the doorposts shook, and the temple was filled with smoke.

Then, without an altar call and without anyone urging him to do so, Isaiah cried out in repentance: "Woe is me! I am lost, for I am a man of unclean lips, and I live among a people of unclean lips."

Isaiah was saying much more than "I've got a dirty mouth." In Matthew 12:34 Jesus declares, "Out of the abundance of the heart the mouth speaks." In confessing the condition of his mouth Isaiah was in fact making a confession about his heart. He did not make excuses or attempt to justify himself before God. Instead he identified with his people group and told the truth about himself and about them.

He confessed that he was a product of his generation and had been socialized to talk and think and believe a certain way.

This clarity came to him as a result of being in worship where God was exalted and magnified. Whenever we truly see God for who God is, the light of his glory causes us to look more closely at ourselves and take a more careful inventory of our life. It is almost as if the glory of God functions like a searchlight or a spotlight that helps us to see things about our people group and ourselves that we hadn't seen or acknowledged before.

This is what it means to worship God in spirit and in truth. It is responding to the Holy Spirit by becoming transparent, honest, humble and vulnerable enough to tell God the truth about the people we represent and about ourselves. In a crosscultural conversation with a Samaritan woman in John 4:19-23, Jesus makes it explicitly clear that these are the kind of worshipers the Father seeks—people who will be honest with God and themselves as an act of true worship. These worshipers are not overly identified with the customs and traditions of their religious or ethnic group. Instead they recognize God as the One who transcends human religious practices and who deserves our true worship and allegiance.

God established himself as the one true God worthy of our worship through the crucifixion and resurrection of Jesus Christ. By dying and rising, the incarnate Son of God put to death all ethnic, racial, religious and national self-worship. No race or ethnicity, nation or religious group can claim any special status. At the cross the basis of all self-worship and pride was destroyed.

When we repent at the foot of the cross, we celebrate Jesus' victory over the pretend rulers of humanity. As we continue to renounce their rule over us in worship, we acknowledge our need for God's help, provision, forgiveness and guidance. Ethnocentrism and racism are forms of idolatry in which we make ourselves the center of our affection and admiration. But when we worship our focus, attention and affection are redirected to God, away from ourselves. In worship no person or group can boast; instead we recognize that we are all the same, and we are humbled. We are no longer the center of our world—God is.

When we look to God and choose to worship and fear him instead of worshiping and fearing people and governments, we proclaim that the empire that oppresses and destroys people is about to fall. We also call people to come out from under the rule of this oppressive empire in order to be in relationship with God. Ideally, this is what Christian worship is supposed to do.

WORSHIP AS WARFARE

Theologian and author Marva Dawn describes how particular aspects of Christian worship should function as instruments of spiritual warfare against the powers and principalities.

Christian worship involves many dimensions of the community's work in relation to the powers. Ideally, the sermon should name them and demonstrate their perversions. The offering attacks the power of money. The intercessory prayers remind us of our task to be agents of God's reconciliation and commit us to live out our faith in Christ's victory over the powers. The sacraments of baptism and the Eucharist give signs and seals that we participate in the triumph of Christ so that the powers have no ultimate control over us. Karl Barth calls this the "priestly function of the Church."[3]

This type of worship focuses us on the kingdom that is "already but not yet," God's multicultural, multilingual, multinational kingdom of justice and love. Worship like this prepares our hearts to receive healing, orders our souls to become like what we adore, renews our minds to envision what God is bringing and begins to make actual the kingdom that is to come.

This perspective is consistent with the teachings of the apostle Paul, and for that matter, those of Jesus Christ, who could never have proclaimed the individualistic, noncontextual, secularized, merely interpersonal messages that we preach in our churches today. Paul always discerned the ruling principalities and powers and proclaimed the gospel in light of those enslaving idolatries. He could no more have had people pray a naive, individualistic, merely interpersonal prayer of salvation than he could have closed his eyes to the larger dimensions of life—visible and invisible. Paul baptized people into a new kingdom with a new ruler and *out of an old kingdom with competing powers*. Paul preached that in baptism people die with Christ to all those enslaving powers and so they are no longer in bondage to them. How could the good news be *good* or *news* otherwise?

The early church understood this. They had a three-year catechumen process to ready new converts for Lent, the time of spiritual discernment and battle, which concluded with baptisms. The early church recognized that baptism symbolizes death to the old way of life and rising to a new way of life. This new way of life includes holy choices to abandon the sins of the flesh, but it also embraces a holy freedom from the ways of the world and the works of Satan.

Unfortunately, when we baptize people today, we merely proclaim that people are cleansed from sin. We are not practicing biblical exorcism, which leads to freedom from demonic powers and principalities. As a result people rise up to avoid sin and to obey Jesus, but they remain totally ignorant of the false ways they have worshiped and of Jesus' power to deliver them from the things that have enslaved them. Consequently, many well-meaning Christians have no idea that they are supposed to live counterculturally, as living representatives of a kingdom made up of people from every tribe, every language and every nation. They have never been confronted with the truth that their racism and ethnocentric attitudes and behaviors demean this kingdom message and are thus contrary to authentic Christian faith and spirituality.

We need to recover this important dimension of our salvation in our day and be empowered and equipped by the Spirit to receive healing and help in our work for love, justice and reconciliation in the earth.

The Holy Spirit is central to the transformation of our lives. Anyone who wants to be healed in his or her ethnic identity needs the work of the Spirit. To be agents of reconciliation, we must learn to practice the presence of God. The profound Christian writer C. S. Lewis understood this:

What is concrete and immaterial can be kept in view only by painful effort.

That is why the real problem of the Christian life comes where people do not usually look for it. It comes the very moment you wake up each morning. All your wishes and hopes (and hurts and hates!) for the day rush at you like wild animals. And the first job each morning consists in shoving them all back; in listening to that other voice, taking that other point of view, letting that other larger, stronger, quieter life come flowing in. And so on, all day. . . . We can do it only for moments at first. But from those moments the new sort of life will be spreading through our system because now we are letting Him work at the right part of us.[4]

Imagine how practicing the presence of God could transform our quest for ethnic healing and racial reconciliation! The "wild animals" of racial superiority, judgment, woundedness, hatred and rage would all be accessible to the melting, piercing presence of God. That quieter, stronger life could get at the right parts of us. That higher perspective could become our perspective. And all this becomes possible as we worship the Holy Spirit—God's transforming presence with us and within us.

In worship the Holy Spirit is intensified and magnified in our lives. It is similar to the way children play with a magnifying glass on a hot summer day. They discover that holding a leaf or piece of paper directly under the magnifying glass allows sunlight to be concentrated and intensified on that object. After a while the heat increases until the leaf or piece of paper is burned up. This is exactly what happens when we worship. The presence and power of God is magnified or intensified to such a degree that the consuming fire of the Holy Spirit burns up anything that is unlike God.

This is why worship is a powerful act of spiritual warfare and racial and ethnic reconciliation. When we worship, we magnify God, and his presence and power advance and expand in our midst. At the same time, in the atmosphere of worship, attitudes and practices that are unlike God are consumed.

CLEANSING WORSHIP

In 1998 people who attended a racial reconciliation conference in Jackson, Mississippi, experienced this phenomenon. Chris Rice and Spencer Perkins—coauthors of the book *More Than Equals*—hosted this outstanding conference. Afterward many of the conference delegates commented on the spiritual intensity of the worship services. Here is what one group said:

> Cynicism, hopelessness, tiredness, despair are major weapons of warfare against us. What made this conference such a powerful experience was the Presence of Christ. There was lots of praise music—lots of worship. *It felt like the worship cleaned the room of darkness, so that everybody could talk. It swept away the defensiveness.* There was a strong sense of God's presence. We saw everything in a whole new way. Where there is light it exposes the darkness. Everything we did began and ended with worship. It was a life-changing experience. We could relate without fear and garbage. It was a God-centered approach to racial reconciliation, and it was where people's "conversion" took place.

Worship exalts, highlights and magnifies God. Worship restores God to his rightful place. Like the prophet Isaiah, we see God high and exalted above all other gods—including our ethnic or racial group and ourselves. God becomes preeminent. Worship restores the balance between knowing that we are the creatures and God is the almighty Creator. We cannot remain proud and arrogant in his presence.

Worship requires us to step out of our comfort zones and enter into the presence of the Holy Spirit, where he is in control. It takes vulnerability to step out on faith and experience God. A posture of humility and vulnerability is cultivated as we enter into the intimacy of worship. In this place God shows us our heart and sends hot coals from the altar to purify and refine us. In worship we get a right view of God, others and ourselves, and we are challenged to put away our idols and acknowledge again that he is the one true and living God, whose kingdom will hold sway throughout all the earth.

We invite you to commit yourself to a lifestyle of worship, the first step in the spiritual process necessary to participate with God in the healing of people and the healing of nations. When we worship our God, we become countercultural communities of life and reconciliation. When we have entered this kind of liberating and life-giving worship, we are ready for the renewal of our mind about our ethnic identity.

The following prayer for being filled with the Holy Spirit is excerpted from Leanne Payne's fine book *Listening Prayer*. We commend it to you as we begin this journey together into spiritual and racial healing. We encourage you to pause now and ask that you may receive the Holy Spirit afresh, as your act of worship.

Come, Holy Spirit, come.
Pour the living water of your presence
On the thirsty ground of my heart.

Make rivers of living water flow
On the barren heights of my soul,
And springs well up within all its valleys.

I would receive power, Lord Jesus Christ, to be your witness
At home and throughout the earth.

Be Thou in me the fountain of living water,
Springing up into everlasting life.

You have qualified me, Holy Father, to share in the inheritance
Of the saints in the kingdom of light.
You have rescued me from the dominion of darkness
And brought me into the kingdom of your dear Son
In whom I have redemption,
The forgiveness of sins (Colossians 1).
You have set your seal upon me,
Your Spirit in my heart as a deposit,
Guaranteeing what is to come.
In Christ, I stand firm (2 Corinthians 1:21-22).
For my adoption in you, I give you thanks.
For this I praise your holy, gracious name.

And I praise you as the one who sends forth your Spirit
Upon those who trust in your name:
"Thou the anointing Spirit art
Who dost thy sev'n-fold gifts impart." (Veni Creator)

I ask you now for the baptism of the Holy Spirit,
And a full freedom to move in the power of your Spirit
To the glory of your Name and the advancement of your kingdom.
I know, Lord, that the day is coming when
"the earth will be filled with the knowledge of the glory
of the Lord, as the waters cover the sea" (Hebrews 2:14).
I rejoice in this, and ask that even now, your Spirit
Will fill me, cover me, and clothe me in this way.
I ask, also, for the grace and strength to so walk before you
That your Holy Spirit will in no way be grieved or offended,

But will remain upon me; be ever pleased to rest upon me.

Father, for this baptism of your Spirit,
One that will continue to well up from within me
And flow out through me,
I give thanks in advance.

It is in Jesus' holy name that I pray and receive this blessing. Amen.[5]

6

EMBRACING OUR
TRUE SELVES

At the end of each one of our racial healing seminars we invite anyone who desires prayer to come forward to receive individual prayer ministry. After one seminar Rick had the privilege of praying for three men; they were quite different from each other, but the need of all three was exactly the same. None of them had learned to embrace their true ethnic identity in Christ. All three were living out of an unreal identity, or false self, and this was severely limiting their ability to embrace racial and ethnic reconciliation.

The first person was Steve, a Chinese American student who was suffering because he felt very distant from God's love and approval. He said, "You must understand, Rick, I am number one son. I must succeed as a doctor. My parents wouldn't feel honored or respected if I did anything less, but I don't think I will be able to do it. I study all the time, but my grades just aren't good enough. I live with the anxiety of it all the time. I've even thought of taking my life. I sometimes feel like it's the only way out for me."

Afterward a young African American man came forward and said, "I grew up in a black middle-class neighborhood. I will never forget the first time a white classmate called me a nigger. I couldn't understand why he said it with such hatred for me. As a child I felt like there must be something wrong with me to justify his anger. I think that event crystallized in me the sense of shame that my daddy had and that I carry, even to this day, in being black."

Then Mike, an Irish American young man, poured out his heart to Rick as they prayed together: "You know, our society is always blaming white males. I'm a white male. I always feel blamed. I always feel mistrusted, just because I'm white. When minority people share the hurts they have suffered, I always feel like saying, 'Hey, I have hurts too! I grew up without a dad. I haven't had an easy time. What did I do to cause racial oppression anyway? It all happened so long ago.'"

All three of these people have been negatively affected by the words and false expectations of others who tried to define their lives. Every day we all—consciously or unconsciously—receive false messages that attempt to define us and tell us who we are. As these messages penetrate our heart, we develop a false self-identity that influences how we view others and ourselves.

God wants to replace those false words with the truth about who we are. We are made in the image of God, and the words we speak have the power to produce life or death in the lives of one another. It is God's intention that we encourage one another toward becoming a glorious new creation, as C. S. Lewis eloquently expressed it in his essay "The Weight of Glory":

> It is a serious thing to live in a society of possible gods and goddesses, and to remember that the dullest and most uninteresting person you can talk to may [be becoming] a creature which, if you saw it now, you would be strongly tempted to worship, or else a horror and a corruption such as you meet, if at all, only in a nightmare. All day long we are, in some degree, helping each other to one or other of these destinations.[2]

False identities are just as ultimately unreal and insubstantial as true identities are eternal and substantial. Lewis points out that the new self is the true self, the real identity of a Christian.

To help us understand idolatry, Lewis used the image of being "bent" toward a person or thing. The idolatrous position is the bent-over position. Rather than standing straight up to reach toward God in worship and so receive true identity from God, we bend in false worship toward other things and people to get an identity from them. We can bend toward money, sex, power, parents, a boyfriend or girl-friend, a husband or wife, a role, a particular culture, a gender or a sexual orientation to get our ultimate identity. We tend to ask these people or things to tell us who we are and to tell us we're okay. When we bend toward other people or things to get an identity, we make those people or things our idols. They replace God at the center of our attention.

To become reconcilers whom God can use to heal people and nations, we must reclaim our uniqueness as ethnic and racial people whose identity is firmly rooted in who God says we are. Unfortunately, however, most Christians have not been taught how to embrace and affirm their cultural heritage and ethnic identity. Instead, unknowingly we have been discipled out of this part of our lives, taught that it is unimportant to our faith. This kind of religious socialization leaves us feeling indifferent about our ethnic identity at best and embarrassed, guilty or confused about our particular value as an ethnic person at worse. The end result is that people are unable to participate in reconciliation efforts to heal people and nations, because it is impossible to affirm in other people something you cannot affirm in yourself.

In Ephesians 4:22-24 the apostle Paul addresses this issue of identity, knowing that how we see ourselves has direct implications for our behavior: "You were taught to put away your former way of life, your old self, corrupt and deluded by its lusts, and to be renewed in the spirit of your minds, and to clothe yourselves with the new self, created according to the likeness of God in true righteousness and holiness." We got a new self, which is our true self, through our union with Christ. God has made his home in us. We are his new temple—individually and corporately. When the Spirit took up residence in us, God made union with us, and now "another lives in us," as Leanne Payne says in *The Healing Presence*.[3]

This is the secret of the Christian life. At the heart of who we are as Christians is a new being, a new creation, produced by the union of God's Spirit with our spirit. This is the determining fact of our existence and the basis of our new identity. We get it as a gift. We merely need to choose to see it, to embrace it, to live in the reality of what we already are and have already been given.

Of course it takes all of our effort to live in that reality, because the false identities within us get much attention and nurture from the world around us and from the prince of this world system, the devil. Therefore to begin the process of embracing our true selves, we must first recognize, renounce and repent of the false identities that have been used to define us.

THE SELF-HATRED IDENTITY

The symptom you will notice if you live in this identity is that you commonly experience a wish to belong to some other ethnicity or race. You envy others' opportunities or self-confidence. Underneath the envy and the wish to be somebody else is a deep rejection of your own self and your own identity.

Self-acceptance is a great human and Christian virtue. It is the recognition that you are created in the image of God and that you are ultimately good. You have intrinsic worth because God made you. Further, God gave you and your people—your ethnic group—the gifts and capacities to create a culture that brings glory to God.

The converse of this is self-hatred, which is a fundamental rejection of the person God made you to be. This is a sin that must be recognized and confessed. Just as women who want to be men are rejecting the good and beautiful creation of God, so you, if you reject or despise your birthright and background, are rejecting and despising the good and beautiful creation of God.

For people who have experienced oppression or conquest, the temptation toward self-hatred is great. It involves internalizing the curse and conquest that another sinful culture and people group perpetrated against your culture and people. In the United States, it has primarily been European American peoples who have subjugated or destroyed people of color. So self-hatred is especially a temptation for people of color.

The first step in coming out of self-hatred is recognizing it for the sin that it is and the false self that it often becomes. In order to do this, we must admit that we have rejected ourselves and our ethnic background and culture. We continue by confessing that we have fed a false self or identity, and then we renounce that false identity by confessing that we are the good creation of God.

It is a glorious thing to watch people of color who have internalized a sense of rejection and even hatred of their background begin to come free and stand up with dignity. This is the dignity God accords to all cultures and ethnicities; each in unique ways becomes an expression of his glory and image in the world.

THE RAGE-FILLED IDENTITY

The other side of the self-hatred coin is the rage-filled identity. These two false identities are never far apart. People often carry these identities together, and they are usually interwoven.

One response to oppression and injustice is to reject and even hate ourselves, thinking we deserve the horrifying treatment we have received. The other pole is to become filled with rage and hatred toward the person or group who has caused us such suffering. Tragically, we always become what we hate. Hatred merely fuels a never-ending cycle of violence and revenge.

The symptom you will notice if you live in this identity is an unexpectedly intense angry response to little things done by people of other ethnicities. You find yourself getting disproportionately angry at every small perceived slight or expression of ignorance. You tend to take it personally and spend lots of time focused on what the person said, what it meant and how you can respond to assert your dignity again.

We want to be clear here. Anger at racism and at the ignorance of European American people is profoundly healthy and right. The issue here is not healthy anger and indignation at injustice. The issue is living in a false identity, characterized by rage.

Both the self-hatred identity and the rage-filled identity have idolatry at the root. Both are identities that come from *being bent toward white people*. When we live out of this identity, we give white people too much power in defining who we are. Then we spend our whole life responding, trying to get white people to repent or make restitution—or ultimately, if those responses are not forthcoming, to get back at white people, to get revenge. This is not a healthy way to spend one's life!

This issue of the false identity of rage has not been understood very well. Progressive people of good intentions have justified the false identity of the rage-filled person on the basis of the evil history of slavery, racism, genocide of Native American people, hatred of Asians during World War II and of Arab people after 9/11. However, the rage-filled identity is destructive to our true identity and to our very life. Vengeance belongs to God alone. God alone can judge rightly. It is not that we let people off the hook, excusing their sins and evil toward others. But we leave balancing the scales to God, and we learn, for our own sake and the sake of the world, even to love our enemy.

Miroslav Volf, a Croatian theologian, understands well the futility, self-destructiveness and ultimately world-destroying power of the rage-filled identity. He writes:

The poor must be delivered from the vengeance and hatred that grips their heart. And then the kingdom of God comes into the world. Jesus confronted the ideology of the rich that invariably blames the victim for their sin and unworthiness. But he also called the poor to repentance for envy and enmity. Envy and enmity transform the ideas of the dominant into the dominant ideas. It is the way that the poor internalize the ideas of the rich, being seduced by their power that enslaves the poor to the dominant system. The poor do not want a new game but only a stronger hand.[4]

We can long for justice and for the judgment of those who have done evil, but in the end we must leave that judgment to God. Rage can only be handled at the cross of Christ. The cross of Christ alone is big enough to take the full expression of all the hurt, hatred, anger and rage we can pour out. Rage belongs above all in God's presence; only there can it be transformed into the humility, holy anger and irrational love of the enemy that God can use in the world.

So we take our rage to the cross. We confess our longing for justice and our appropriate anger, and we admit and confess our hatred of others as a violence that reinforces sin. We continue by naming the rage-filled identity as a false and destructive identity, and we take our rage into the presence of God and express it to Jesus on the cross.

THE VICTIM IDENTITY

Although people have been and are being systematically victimized in America, we live in a society in which people and groups seem to compete or vie for victim status. If a person or group can find a way to claim that they are victims, they have a right to justice and restitution and have found a basis for political clout.

Unfortunately, victims are not responsible for themselves and their plight. They must always look to others to fix the situation. They are dependent on the actions and choices of others for making their life better. In that sense, they are bent over toward the person who caused the problem and is now expected to fix it. The victim identity is another subtle form of idolatry toward people who have misused and abused their power.

Persons who are living in this identity often feel sad or depressed when they are alone and have nothing to distract them. They also may choose to mask their pain and find temporary comfort through food, alcohol, sex or some other addictive pleasurable experience. Although this may bring some short-term relief, neither depression nor addiction can bring about transformation.

There are different ways people can establish themselves in a victim role. A healthy person may use history as evidence that perpetrators indeed owe repentance and restitution to the people they have sinned against. However when this use of history is no longer helpful, they can let go of that approach and take responsibility for their own life and destiny. John Perkins, a leading author and pioneer in racial reconciliation and Christian urban redevelopment, has been able to do this type of adjustment in a masterful way. Rick observed this firsthand when he accompanied Dr. Perkins to a white church where he preached about the devastating effects of racism and injustice and called the church to take responsibility, give generously, and pursue the basic principles of Christian community development—reconciliation, relocation and redistribution. Afterward Perkins went to a black church to preach. The message in this context was *very* different. He called the people to take responsibility for their lives and to face the painful wounds, brokenness and sin in the black community. He challenged them: "You don't expect the people who got you into this mess to get you out, do you? We need to take responsibility. We must not allow ourselves to be dependent on somebody else or on some other group. Solving our problems is up to us, with God's help."

In order to come out of the victim mentality and identity, we must begin just as we would when renouncing other false identities. We start by confessing that we have seen ourselves as victims without any power to change our situation. We continue by agreeing that we have embraced the lie of the enemy of our soul—the lie that other groups have dominance or superiority over our racial or ethnic group. It is not true that a person or group cannot get ahead or succeed because a certain group of people tends to see them as inferior. We do not have to live into that reality and thus produce a self-fulfilling prophecy. Instead our ethnic identity can be healed and restored through Jesus Christ, and we can be strengthened by the Holy Spirit to choose the good and not be trapped in addictive, self-destructive behaviors. So the healing process begins with awareness, confession and renouncing the lie of our powerlessness.

THE MODEL MINORITY IDENTITY

Any person of color who succeeds in America can be tempted to take on this false identity. The symptom you will notice if you are taking on this identity is that you feel shame and great awkwardness when you are around relatives and other people of your cultural background who are acting especially "ethnic" and traditional. You feel much greater affinity with white European Americans and a sense of shame about your parents or grandparents. You have an inordinate desire to fit in and be accepted by the dominant group. You may see it as your responsibility to be a positive role model for your entire racial or ethnic group or to dispel negative stereotypes about your people by performing at high levels.

This shame-based behavior must be faced and your background must be embraced if you are to make peace with yourself as a bicultural person. Although you may appear quite competent, the false identity of the model minority is another way for people of color to bend toward white European Americans, another way to internalize racism. The call for you is to be genuinely bicultural and to embrace the whole of your ethnic and cultural inheritance. Then when white European Americans compliment you for being so unlike others from your racial or ethnic background, you will set a boundary for them, making it clear that you are not complimented by such an aspersion cast on others.

It is also important that you release your feelings of shame about your ethnic heritage or your parents and grandparents at the cross of Christ. Ask God for the grace to value and embrace your heritage. Jesus wants to take the burden that you are carrying to speak for and represent your people. No one should have to bear that kind of pressure. As you ask God to lift off the burden and the need to prove your worth by what you accomplish, he can set you free from the performance anxiety and perfectionism that often accompany this false identity.

THE HIP WHITE PERSON IDENTITY

In this day of political correctness and increased social tolerance, there are European Americans who base their identity on being the white person who gets it. They would like to be perceived as hip, cool individuals who can be trusted by people of color. Through their language, clothing, mannerisms and social networks, they suggest that they have understood their white privilege, have rejected it, and now are committed to giving their lives to serve people of color in their quest for justice, power and equality.

This false identity reveals a white person's bentness toward people of color. It is the attempt of European American people to become or be identified as "black" or "Hispanic," usually out of shame or guilt about their own culture. They attempt to achieve this by immersing themselves in the identity of another group. Their sense of worth is based on the acceptance they receive from the particular group they are trying to identify with.

A person wrapped up in this false identity almost never says anything good about being European American and is very critical of their culture and ethnicity. For them whiteness has become a symbol only of injustice, undeserved privilege and the evil of racism. Interestingly, this false identity seems to be a particular temptation for people who, for one reason or another, felt alienated from European American culture and values while they were growing up.

Ironically, people of color can often sense it when a European American person is alienated from their own ethnic identity. As a result people of color, who have often struggled to regain their own healthy sense of ethnic pride and self-acceptance, tend to mistrust this person's motives. Some people of color may use this shame-and-guilt-based identity for their own purposes or to further a particular political agenda or a social cause, but ultimately these relationships will not be based on respect for the person with the false identity.

In the instances when people of color do embrace and respect the white person who is seeking acceptance, that person will still be alienated from a very important part of who they are—their European American heritage. It is important that white Americans identify with and repent of the sinful, fallen aspects of their culture. However, it is equally important to own and celebrate the positive elements of this ethnic heritage. Although it is true that European and European American culture has been particularly bloodthirsty and prone to dominance, it is also true, for example, that this people group has been unusually open to science and exploration.

We recognize that none of our ethnic ancestors created a perfect culture; rather, in their broken humanity they created fallen societies. Therefore our call to self-acceptance does not imply a blanket embrace of the sinful and fallen aspects of your culture and background. Our challenge to you is to recognize that God has deposited some of his image in every people group and that he intends to use your ethnicity and culture as a vehicle to express his glory.

THE WHITE SUPERIORITY IDENTITY

Though we sadly suspect that very few people who consciously embrace this false identity will read this book, it is important to include it because this false identity has influenced our culture in profound ways. Anti-Semitism, slavery, Native American genocide, Jim Crow segregation laws, the Holocaust in Germany in World War II, Japanese internment camps and the conquest of the American Southwest are all rooted in this false self. In addition, hate groups are on the rise and the Internet has become a powerful tool to help these groups recruit new followers and connect them to a worldwide network. The rise of these groups suggests that there are many in our nation who live in this false identity.

We all notice particularly exaggerated and vehement expressions of this false self, but it is important to recognize that some very subtle forms of the white supremacist false identity infect all European Americans. This attitude and mindset has been so endemic throughout our history that it is passed on to white children from their parents and grandparents like a virus. It means that when they see a person of color, they tend to make judgments without knowing anything about that person. It affects the way values are developed and promoted. This consequence can be seen in the disparities in U.S. educational systems of America and in the way white Americans can explain away the numbers of black and Latino men in prison while making no connection to the real effects of being poor and undereducated in this country.

The question is often asked whether people of color can be racists. We contend that ethnocentrism—the belief that one's ethnic group is central and superior—has characterized many ethnic groups throughout history, and therefore anyone can be ethnocentric. However, *racism*—the belief that my race is inherently superior and destined to dominate—is a peculiarly European and European American construct. The evil of racism is an expression of the sin of self-worship whose roots go back to Europe. Racism is the European and American form of "racialized" ethnocentrism. Europeans and their descendants used racial differences as a pretext to unite Europeans and their descendants in efforts to gain and keep global power. Racial categorizing was not common among the cultures of the world until European scientists and leaders made it central.[5]

To become people who can participate in God's work of healing people and healing nations, then, European Americans must intentionally renounce this false identity and repent of it for the sin that it is. Exodus 34:7 teaches us that the sins of the parents will be visited on their descendants to the fourth generation. In American history that takes us back to before the Civil War. Unconfessed and unrenounced false identities persist across generations, with consequences that we can't even imagine. Most people of color know that our society is still profoundly racist in its attitudes, structures and systems, but many European Americans remain blissfully unaware of how the false identity of white superiority pervasively affects our society today.

We have heard many people say that "those things" (slavery, Native American genocide, internment and so on) happened a long time ago. But the passage of time does nothing to forgive sin and heal the wounds caused by it. Only confession, renunciation and the cleansing, liberating power of the cross can heal us and free us from the devastating generational bondage of our past.

We are convinced that if European Americans would confess the sinful idolatry of white superiority, renounce it and repent of it, God would pour out his blessing on our country in a powerful way. As white Americans humbly renounce this false identity, may God begin to pour out waves of healing upon our nation, freeing us from this destructive generational bondage that has lasted much too long.

THE COLOR-BLIND IDENTITY

Many white people in our society don't think of themselves as being ethnic at all. They may not know their European ethnic background, or if they do, it is so mixed that they can't identify with any particular ethnicity. People who live in this identity may say, "I don't see a person's skin color. I don't think that matters at all." Or, "I'm not prejudiced. Some of my best friends are _____ [fill in the appropriate ethnic group]." These comments, though they may be expressed with the best of intentions, are not helpful. They show ignorance and lack of awareness more than they communicate love and acceptance.

Although skin color does not matter genetically, it has mattered a great deal historically. Ignoring it or waving away historical realities by making facile comments about prejudice and racism is not a path toward genuine racial and ethnic reconciliation. Until we know who we are ethnically, we are unable to really reconcile genuinely with others. And until we know and recognize people for who they really are—including some of their history as a people—and then interact with them in ways that actually influence how we see ourselves, we cannot genuinely reconcile with them.

Therefore, a crucial first step in ethnic healing and reconciliation for white Americans is to own their own background and face what people of their ethnicity have done toward others. We begin this process by acknowledging that being a white American is an ethnic identity. It is actually an identity that is quite strongly supported in American culture. In fact, this identity has so much support that we don't need to recognize it in order to benefit from it. The "I am not an ethnic person" identity is a false identity. It allows white Americans to enjoy the privileges and reinforcement of their ethnic identity without owning the injustices that have resulted for people with other identities. When naive or insensitive comments are made out of this false self, whites need to admit that, turn from it, and ask God to help them come to terms with the ethnic person they are. This frees those in the dominant culture to embrace the good aspects of the white American identity and renounce those that are destructive.

Whites need to identify with the positive achievements of Western culture. This culture has been idealistic, democratic, scientific, individualistic, economically successful, technological, entrepreneurial and expansive. However, whites must also identify with the sins of Western culture. This culture has pursued economic and military conquest, sought to win at any cost, and used science and technology to make war and manipulate governments. White Americans have been blindly individualistic and rejected all corporate responsibility for sins against other people groups. Western governments and corporations are the world champions at spin doctoring and spin control and have created a pleasing but false image of themselves for export around the world.

In order to be free of their false identity, whites must choose to identify with both the good and the bad and take responsibility for their cooperation in corporate and historical expressions of evil and sin. Positive and negative dimensions of white ethnicity are inescapable for white Americans and must be faced and embraced so that the false identity can be renounced and replaced.

OTHER FALSE IDENTITIES

We have tried to cover the false identities that are particularly common in our culture. Other false characterizations of people of various ethnic groups and cultural backgrounds, however, can also harm their sense of worth and self-esteem. For example, African American men have been demonized and demeaned in our culture as either comical and accommodating or angry and dangerous. This translates into stereotypes that portray them as entertainers, criminals or warrior athletes. Since these images are so pervasive in our society, they can subliminally influence young black boys to limit their aspirations or to develop a negative false self based on one of these identities.

Hispanic people in our culture can be seen as hot-tempered, hot-blooded people who tend to be violent or sexually unrestrained. Such misperceptions and stereotypes are particularly dangerous for Latina women, who could be deemed easy prey to unwanted sexual advances of men who see women as commodities.

Likewise, because of the brutal treatment of Native American people in North America, overwhelming problems of unemployment and homelessness have led to widespread depression and despair in this community. Instead of addressing the social problems that have virtually destroyed this people group, white Americans often attribute a destructive false identity to Native American men as alcoholics and lazy individuals. Being perceived in such negative ways has taken its toll on many lives in the Native American community.

Finally, European Americans are sometimes seen as cold-hearted, money-hungry workaholics who would sell their mother to make a buck. This too is a false identity; it can produce a "what's the use?" attitude, social paralysis and feelings of guilt that can never be assuaged.

None of these false identities is who God says we are; all of them are ultimately unreal, not true, insubstantial and destructive. So if you are Asian you can embrace your ancestry and cultural heritage with dignity. Your wisdom and generous hospitality are gifts from God, as are the beauty, style and soul of the African American culture. Native Americans' spirituality and sensitivity to the harmony of all things reflect the image of God, as do the passion and loyalty of Latino peoples and the vision and entrepreneurial spirit of Europeans.

Even if your ethnic background has not shaped you in these particular ways, in all likelihood you have inherited strengths from your culture that are important to give thanks for and to contribute to others. Celebrate who God has made you to be and give thanks for the goodness, beauty and dignity of your ethnic ancestors and cultural background.

RENOUNCING AND REPENTING OF FALSE IDENTITIES

Now that we have uncovered some of Satan's false characterizations and begun to embrace our true self, we must complete the work by renouncing and repenting of these false identities. We do this by praying and confessing the truth about our heritage before God and each other. We admit our bent-over position and choose with our wills to stand straight up and receive the blessing of our true self that only Christ can give. In his presence we listen for his healing word— his word of freedom from the false self.

The following prayers are focused on the strengthening of our will to help us enter into his presence and confess the idolatry that has caused us to be bent toward others for our sense of worth and identity. The first and most important step in reclaiming our true self is to stand up and look to Christ for our identity. Once we do this, we will find that our key need is for the strengthening of the will to live out of our true identity. The bent-over position weakens the will and accustoms it to dependency and passivity. So when we stand up out of our bentness and embrace our true identity, we ask God to strengthen our weak will so that we can choose obedience again—

obedience to celebrate and embrace the good in our ethnic identity and heritage.

Begin this process by praying the following prayers to renounce your false identity and embrace your true self in Christ. These prayers can be prayed alone or with a group. However, it would be a mistake to jump too quickly into leading groups using these prayers. Only after God has led your own soul through the process can you lead others. You must learn the skill of listening to God and must also have experienced some real transformation in these areas of your life if you are to have the wisdom to lead others well.

To begin, please place your hand over your heart and pray.[6]

I thank you, Lord Jesus, that you are one with the Father, that the Father is one with you, and that you are one with me. I thank you that you and the Father have made your home in me. Another lives in me! Thank you, Lord. Praise you that you, who flung stars into space, now hold my heart in your loving hands. Thank you that you live in me to transform me. Thank you, Jesus!

I pray, Lord, for the release and strengthening of my will, that with which I initiate change and choose life, and with which I forsake the bent, idolatrous position of attempting to find my identity in other people or other things.

Show me any way in which I am bent toward the creature. O Lord, reveal any idolatrous dependency on persons or things, show me any way in which I demand from the created the identity I can gain only from you, my Creator.

In silence, invite the Lord to bring to your mind any images that might help you visualize how you may be bent toward other people for your identity. Sit with this image for a while. Then see yourself deliberately straightening up, away from that idol, as you pray the following prayer:

I choose, Lord, to forsake this bent position toward other people. I confess it to you, just now, as the sin of idolatry that it is. I renounce it in your name, and I thank you for your forgiveness. I open myself now to receive your forgiveness and cleansing.

Now that you have renounced the false identity that sought to define you, continue with a prayer of dedication to strengthen your will.

Come into me, divine, initiating, eternal Will. Lord, command what you will and then will what you command.

I thank you, Lord, that my weak and insufficient will is now one with yours. May I know more and more what it means to be in-willed, indwelt by you. Thank you, Lord, that you are completing the healing work you have begun in me and you will continue it in this world and the next.

God, fill me now with your light and your love. Replace the empty places that were filled with distorted images and dependent relationships. Fill me with your presence, with your light, with images of the good and the true and the beautiful. Spirit of God, now fill me from the bottom of my toes to the top of my head, fill every cell of my being with your presence. Come, Holy Spirit. Fill me and use me, I pray, for I give you all thanks and all glory and all praise.

I choose now to meet my God-given needs in God-glorifying and health-giving ways. And I ask, Lord, that you teach me to minister to others in the way you are now ministering to me. For I pray in your name. Amen.

FOLLOW-UP ACTIVITIES FOR INDIVIDUALS OR GROUPS

1. Review the list of false identities below, and reflect in your journal on which of these false selves have most characterized or influenced you.

- ☐ Self-hatred identity
- ☐ Rage-filled identity
- ☐ Victim identity
- ☐ Model minority identity
- ☐ Hip white person identity
- ☐ White superiority identity
- ☐ Color-blind identity
- ☐ Any other false identities received from your ethnic background

2. Spend time praying aloud specifically for your involvement in this false identity. Pray aloud where you are now. If you are in a group, it will be best if people can go forward to acknowledge a particular false identity and be prayed for by a prayer minister.

   To one another you can now proclaim forgiveness: "To those who truly repent, I proclaim you forgiven, in Christ's name. Receive this forgiveness now into your heart."

3. In your prayer journal, describe the images of bentness toward others that came to your mind; then converse with God about them. He will give you understanding and help you begin to get at the roots of the idolatries or dependencies that have held you back from full freedom in him.

   Visualize the cross of Christ between you and the person or thing you were bent toward. See Jesus coming between you and that person or group—setting a holy boundary, protecting you from hurtful or dependency-building acts and words.

4. Now celebrate! Give thanks to God for his mighty presence with you and within you.

RECEIVING AND
EXTENDING FORGIVENESS

When Rick was twelve years old, one day he and his brother were attacked by an angry black youth. First the young man hit Rick's brother, then he turned and hit Rick. The brothers were terrified, unable to protect each other, but they were also angry. After several swings and many obscenities, the fight broke up, but it made a lasting impression on Rick, who began to hold a fear in his heart about young black men.

Later, as Rick grew in his commitment to reconciliation and justice, he knew that he had to deal with the memory of this fight and the stereotype of young black men that it reinforced. So during a special prayer time, Rick invited Jesus into this memory. In his mind's eye Rick saw Jesus enter the baseball field where the fight happened, break it up, look at the young black man and speak words of tenderness to break through his defenses.

As Rick watched Jesus, he began to feel the immense woundedness in the young man that had resulted in almost uncontrollable rage, and Rick began to feel compassion. As a result, Rick was empowered by Jesus to extend forgiveness out of a new understanding, to pray for that young man and to ask for God's forgiveness for himself. Jesus cleansed Rick that day and freed him to make a commitment to work for a world where people of color will not have so many reasons for rage.

This experience illustrates the crucial part played by the healing of memories in the process of forgiveness that leads to racial healing and reconciliation. As we saw in the previous chapter, we live in a society where ethnic stereotypes abound, false images that are promoted in the media and through selective news reporting. These stereotypes then take root in our hearts and minds, and if we have personal experiences that reinforce them, they can profoundly distort our relationships. Our corporate history, too, is littered with painful experiences of others' fear and hatred, events that influence and infect our perceptions and relationships to this day. These seemingly distant historical events are reinforced by more recent experiences of police brutality, racial profiling, race riots, hate crimes and a thousand daily examples of discrimination. But God wants to use his people to break through these hostilities and heal the wounds they have inflicted.

Now that we have come into the freedom of embracing our true ethnic identity and renouncing false identities, we are ready to face the immense issue of *sin*. Sin is an enslaving power, according to Paul in Romans 6:1-14. Sin seeks to trap us in a never-ending vicious cycle of self-destructive dominance, revenge and hatred. However, as Rev.

Dr. Martin Luther King Jr. rightly observed, "The doctrine of an eye for an eye can only end in a world gone blind." That's why Christians must find a way of breaking the vicious cycle of sin and counter-sin. It is our belief that only the cross and the forgiveness that the cross makes possible can do that.

In this chapter we will deal with sin, forgiveness, and how to overcome the pride, dominance, rage and revenge that result from racism. If we attempt to build friendships or bring institutional change without addressing these core issues, our efforts will leave immense problems unresolved and festering. Unresolved pain and bitterness that result from unconfessed pride and dominance will unravel friendships and undermine lasting change. Crosscultural trust issues will continue to surface in never-ending and self-defeating ways. We need a spiritual change at the core to sustain high trust levels, empower enduring friendships and bring lasting institutional changes.

Facile, empty acts of forgiveness will not break the negative cycle. Any process that glosses over the full extent and seriousness of the sin and evil done against others by us will fail. Too often people in power have exhorted people under their authority to forgive quickly and automatically, without an adequate change of heart or behavior on the part of the offender. This approach has given forgiveness and the cross a bad name. If the cross means that people in power can act as badly as they wish and then expect that those who have been victimized should extend immediate, automatic forgiveness, then the cross is a farce! It has merely become another tool to reinforce the idolatry of ethnocentrism and racism and the practice of ethnic superiority.

As potential reconcilers who want to bring healing to people and nations, we must understand and embrace genuine forgiveness and authentic racial reconciliation. We have to recover the real power and meaning of the cross—not as the tool for deception and dominance that it has become through Christianity-ism, but as a gateway to healing, reconciliation and revival.

The journey into forgiveness begins with the healing of memories in those areas where we've sinned or been sinned against. The healing of memories takes seriously the impact of sin and evil, names it, makes it visible, and brings Jesus and the power of his cross into the middle of the event or situation that caused pain. Forgiveness through the healing of memories can melt our hearts, but it is not intended as an easy way out. We are to practice the healing of memories in the context of multiethnic communities and gatherings, where the healing that happens is reciprocal and transforming.

It is through the practice of the healing of memories that we invite Jesus to enter into our imaginations to exert his lordship over the past experiences that we have had with each other. Many of us are committed to bring every thought we have under the lordship of Christ. However, often our imaginations and memories are left unredeemed in this process. We believe that Jesus is also the Lord of our imagination and of our memories. Jesus wants to sanctify or cleanse and claim our imagination by speaking into our stereotypical images and our traumatic experiences with one another. The healing of memories, if practiced rightly, can open up a whole new dimension of how our imaginations can be used to apply the power of the cross to the core parts of who we are and how we see one another.

Healing of memories has been practiced now for several decades in ministries of physical and emotional healing. These ministries seek to invite God's presence into traumatic events of the past in order to bring the divine forgiveness of sins to bear on the affected relation-ships. This important approach has rarely been applied to racial rec-onciliation and the fight for justice.

Many people make the healing of memories a very mystical expe-rience. However the heart of the practice is simply to make a full con-fession of sin, related to all our past experiences, and to extend for-giveness to all people who have sinned against us, as individuals and as groups. This is not just a superficial review of the destructive and horrifying history we have shared. Extending forgiveness can happen only when we have taken time to name sin and evil for what it is and to recognize the impact it has had. Extending forgiveness is an abso-lutely essential act for people who have been sinned against. Without such an act, we—and especially people of color—carry rage, resent-ment and self-hatred that can cripple us. We must extend forgiveness for our own sake as much as for the sake of our enemy, even though we realize it may not be received. When we refuse to let go of the debt of dignity and respect that others owe us, we give those others too much power to dominate and determine our life.

The process of extending forgiveness also allows us to bring our hurt, rage and hopelessness into the presence of God and lay it at the foot of the cross. It is only here that we can express all the anger, hurt and despair we feel and not be overwhelmed by it or overwhelm oth-ers. The cross is the only safe place to let the dangerous and destruc-tive depth of our hurt, rage, pain and fear be expressed. So when we pray for people to receive racial healing, we encourage them to ex-press their rage or fear to Christ on the cross—and we have seen mir-acles of healing and restoration.

In order for racial and ethnic reconciliation to become a reality, the healing process must take place personally, in small groups and in larger groups. If we are to build relationships and work together for justice, we must face our past together and allow God to heal us and ultimately send us to bring healing to the nations. As we take this spiritual transformation model out into the world, we will discover that often the historical memories that need to be healed are between younger nations and their European colonial captors—for example, between South Africa and the Netherlands, between Uganda and Great Britain. In other situations the healing of history needs to happen between ethnic groups of a similar racial background, such as between Japanese and Korean people because of Japan's brutal conquest of and rule over Korea for many generations. This dynamic would also apply to the Orthodox Serbs and Catholic Croats in the former Yugoslavia and to Hutus and Tutsis in Rwanda.

It is important to recognize that a global understanding of racial hatred and ethnic strife is critical to our success as reconcilers in this generation. We need more than an individual approach to the process of racial and ethnic reconciliation: there is a need for the collective healing of memories. Racial and ethnic divisions are fraught with historical memories that have seared our consciences and destroyed our moral credibility as nations. These conscience-searing events and experiences must be acknowledged, brought into the light of God's presence, confessed and repented of. As we come together in multi-ethnic gatherings and pursue the healing of memories, the impact of sin and evil is made visible. Forgiveness is received and extended. Then people may be called to pray prayers of blessing over those who have hurt them and over those that they have hurt. These times of blessing and healing are powerful opportunities to welcome the outpouring of God's Spirit in our midst to make real his mighty work of reconciliation through the power of the cross. Such gatherings for healing can become catalysts for a great revival of God's Spirit in his church, as a mighty witness to an unbelieving world.

Experiences and memories that should be examined and worked through in the healing of memories—personally and corporately—are all those that are affecting our present relationships. Some of those experiences and memories are individual. Rick's experience with the young black teenager, recounted at the beginning of this chapter, is an example. However, many experiences are corporate and historical, and they live on in our group memory through retellings of the event and by seeing the consequences of its impact all around us.

For instance, when praying with African American men, Rick finds he often needs to help them pray through how they have been treated in American society. Likewise when praying with Puerto Ricans born on the U.S. mainland, we have found that they often feel great pride in their Puerto Rican culture but have a deep sense of not belonging on the U.S. mainland *or* in Puerto Rico. This sense of alienation is often rooted in specific memories that must be prayed through.

Native Americans have seen alcoholism ravage their families in very personal and destructive ways. European American settlers fostered alcoholism among Native Americans from the early days of colonization. This destructive strategy was one dimension of their plan to commit genocide and is a corporate memory that must be healed by bringing it into the presence of God through prayer. Other historical injustices include the boarding schools that separated First Nations children from their families and their culture, and the lack of community resources on present-day reservations. These corporate and individual memories all have to be brought into the healing presence of Christ.

Another recent example and very present memory for many Asian Americans is the Los Angeles race riots, when African American and Latino residents of the South Central community destroyed millions of dollars worth of Korean American property. The killing of Vincent Chinn by unemployed blue-collar auto workers in Detroit, because he was assumed to be Japanese and Japan's auto industry was luring away the market from American companies, is another tragic example that resonates in the collective memory of Asian Americans.

As we move forward in the healing of memories of racial and ethnic injustice, we must recognize that all of us have participated in some way in racial problems and brokenness, either by our actions or by our silence. In addition, many of us suffer (or enjoy) long-term consequences of unjust choices that our forebears made. For example, white Americans have benefited economically, educationally, politically and socially from the actions of their ancestors. Peggy McIntosh, professor at Wellesley College, calls this invisible advantage enjoyed by white people in our society "white privilege." White privilege includes the following rights that are often taken for granted by those who have them:

- I can arrange to be in the company of people of my race most of the time.

- I can be pretty sure of renting or purchasing housing in an area that I can afford and in which I would want to live.

- I can be pretty sure that my neighbors in such a location will be neutral or pleasant to me.

- I can turn on the television or open the front page of my paper and see people of my race widely and positively represented.

- When I am told about our national heritage or about "civilization," I am shown that people of my color made it what it is.

- I can be sure that my children will be given curricular materials that will testify to the existence of their race.

- Whether I use checks, credit cards, or cash, I can count on my skin color not to work against the appearance of financial reliability.

- I can speak a colloquial language, or dress in second hand clothes, or arrive late to an engagement without having people attribute these choices to the bad morals, poverty or illiteracy of my race.

- I can do well in a challenging situation without being called a credit to my race.

- I am never asked to speak for all the people of my racial group.

- If a traffic cop pulls me over, I can be sure I haven't been singled out because of my race.

- I can choose public accommodation without fearing that people of my race cannot get in or will be mistreated in the places I have chosen.[1]

People of European background have these advantages even though they are often unaware of them and may not have done any-thing to gain them. But as Gordon Marino points out in his article "Me? Apologize for Slavery?" people who benefit from a crime against others share in the responsibility for the crime and need to help make things right even if they didn't have anything to do with the initial criminal act.[2] If I learn that I am rich because my father stole a million dollars from one of his friends, I am responsible for admitting the wrongdoing and trying to make restitution. White Europeans have benefited immensely from the free or cheap labor of people of color over the last several hundred years. If we benefit, we are responsible to admit it and do what we can to make it right.

As Paul teaches us in 1 Corinthians 12, when any member of the body is hurting, we all hurt. Similarly, when any member of Christ's body sins against God and others, we are all affected, and we are all responsible for taking action to restore the perpetrator and make restitution to the victimized. That responsibility begins with God in prayer, and we follow through by allowing God to show us what we must do in response. There may be no greater thing you could do to become an agent of ethnic healing and reconciliation.

Brenda, as a person of color, has herself had to seek healing and forgiveness in interracial relationships. One of her more painful experiences occurred when she spoke at the 2000 Urbana Mission Convention. On the second day of the convention she spoke to twenty thousand people in a plenary session, recounting her church's tragic experience of losing Coach Ricky Birdsong to the bullet of a white member of a hate group who went on a rampage in Chicago and northern Indiana.

When Brenda told this story, she neglected to mention that this hate-filled man had also taken the life of a Korean young man, partly because she was afraid she might mispronounce his name. The Asian Americans, especially Koreans, who were present were deeply hurt by this omission.

The next morning, in front of the whole convention, Brenda went back on stage and confessed. She apologized publicly and asked for forgiveness, especially from the Korean community. Over the next few days she visited Korean gatherings at Urbana. The experience was so deeply humbling for her. Yet the events that had so affected the life of her own church deepened her identification with the pain of Koreans.

Her confession and repentance moved the whole convention. As she asked for forgiveness, she said that as an African American person she now understood how it must feel to be white. She identified with how difficult it must be to try hard to "get it right" but not be able to say or do the right thing.

Through this experience we have learned that through giving and receiving forgiveness we identify with and reach out to the people we have excluded or neglected—and the kingdom of God advances mightily!

How Do We Practice the Healing of Memories?

We can practice the healing of memories of personal and corporate experiences using the following process.

1. We worship God and practice God's presence, confess and celebrate our union with Christ.

2. We ask God to bring to mind memories or images of past relationships or experiences with people of another ethnicity or race. We wait on God until he brings to our mind some image or memory.

3. We invite Jesus into that memory and wait on him to show us how he acts in relation to the event or situation. Jesus was present in

the original experience because Jesus has always been with us, even from the womb. And Jesus can enter into memories and images in our mind now and bring insight and healing. He wants to be Lord of our imagination and to cleanse even the images and memories in our mind. So we wait on Jesus for his insight or action in our mind's eye. In this way we seek to "see" Jesus and his truths and ways with the eyes of our heart. When Rick invited Jesus into the memory of the attack he recounted at the beginning of this chapter, Jesus walked in and protected Rick but also expressed tenderness and understanding to the young African American. God loves us and acts to heal and protect us and to heal and protect others as well. Sometimes that loving response will be expressed in a fresh image that comes to our mind's eye.

If no image or memory comes, we can still continue through the rest of the steps. But often when we wait on Jesus' response to key events and memories, he will show us something that can help us to take the remaining steps in the process of extending and receiving forgiveness.

4. We express the hurt, anger, frustration, hatred and/or fear that we felt toward any person or group that harmed us. We can picture the person in front of us and tell them directly. We can invite the person or group to listen while we tell Jesus our feelings. Then we can choose to extend forgiveness, either asking Jesus to forgive them or speaking words of forgiveness to them ourselves.

Forgiveness is always an act of the will. But it ought to come *after* a clear expression of the depth of our hurt, pain and anger. Otherwise it can be shallow and will likely need to be deepened later. People who are not ready to clearly express the depth of their hurt and anger are often not yet ready to forgive. Extending forgiveness too quickly can be an unhealthy act of denial and self-deprecation. When we are hurt, God gets angry, and it is very healthy for us to get angry too. Then forgiveness can be profound and lasting, because it has come after we've fully recognized the depth and seriousness of the sin's impact.

5. Then we wait on Jesus for insight into the sinful ways we responded to the person's sin against us. As Jesus shows us these sinful responses, we confess them and ask for his cleansing and forgiveness. We may be locked in bitter feelings, or constantly haunted by self-destructive rage; we may have chosen to escape the pain and comfort ourselves with addictive relationships to people or sex or food or alcohol. Or we may have more subtle but sinful responses, like workaholism or perfectionism or always trying to fix other wounded people. We let Jesus show us how we coped and what we need to confess regarding the way we responded to the sin against us.

6. We pray then for the lifting off of any influence of the evil one—Satan and the demonic—that came through the experience. We place the cross between us and the person or group of people who hurt us. The cross becomes a holy boundary of protection but also a holy gateway for relationship.

7. Finally, we pray for God's strength to love in word and deed the person or group of people who wounded us, and we begin by praying God's best for that person or group. And we give thanks to God!

The following set of reflections are designed to lead people through the process of making a full confession, receiving and extending forgiveness, and beginning the ongoing work of changing their thinking, attitudes and behavior by taking personal responsibility in a biblically healthy way. This worksheet can be used as a follow-up activity by an individual or a small group, guiding you into a deeper practice of giving and receiving forgiveness through the healing of memories.

MAKING A FULL CONFESSION

Receiving Cleansing And Healing

HOW HAVE YOU PERSONALLY PARTICIPATED IN OR BEEN AFFECTED BY RACISM and prejudice in our society?

- When have you remained silent or gone along with a conversation in which some ethnic group is put down or made fun of? When have you said or thought things that were belittling or judgmental toward another ethnic group?

- What values, accomplishments or traits tend to make people in your ethnic group feel superior to or better than people in other ethnic groups? How have you accepted these judgments or expressed them yourself?

- How have you been hurt by the racism or prejudice of others, and how would you like God to heal you? In what ways and for what experiences do you need to extend forgiveness?

What sins of your people or your ancestors do you want to confess and repent of, either because their sin still affects you (see Deuteronomy 20:5-6) or because you have benefited in some way from the sins of others in the past and accepted those benefits without any awareness or response?

What sins of the church, of God's people, do you want to confess, repent of and renounce, just as Nehemiah confessed and took responsibility for the sins of God's people (see Nehemiah 1:4-11)?

Do you need to talk with another person to gain the full sense of cleansing, forgiveness, repentance and healing that God wants to give you? (See James 5:13-16 and note the connection between sickness and unconfessed sin.) Whom would you want to seek out for assurance of forgiveness or prayer for healing?

What steps do you want to take to better understand your personal responsibility, to act differently toward others and to more intentionally work for justice?

8

DENOUNCING THE POWERS
AND PRINCIPALITIES

While attending Fuller Theological Seminary in Pasadena, California, Brenda took a class on demonic oppression taught by Dennis Guernsey. This well-respected author, marriage and family therapist, and seminary professor began the class by explaining that at one time he, like most American evangelicals, did not believe in the existence of demons. He was a well-educated man, not the kind of person who looked for a demon under every rock. However, an experience with a client had changed his understanding completely.

A young man he fictitiously called John had come to him for counseling. John confessed to being a born-again Christian who struggled with a perverted sexual addiction. He knew it was wrong, and he felt extremely remorseful and guilty about his behavior—but he couldn't

THE HEART OF RACIAL JUSTICE

stop. Time was running out for him, because the nature of his problem required that, as a licensed therapist, Dr. Guernsey would have to report him to the police. Over the course of their therapeutic relationship, Dr. Guernsey became very fond of John and sincerely wanted to help him overcome his struggle. He tried every therapeutic approach that he could think of, but to no avail.

Finally, one day in exasperation, Dr. Guernsey put his head in his hands and said to John, "I've tried everything I know to do for you and nothing has worked. Do you think this could be a—like a—demon?"

To his shock and amazement, a cursing voice came out of John saying, "It took you long enough, s---head!"

Then Dr. Guernsey underwent a long, difficult spiritual process of trying to minister deliverance and healing to this young man to free him from the demonic forces that had taken hold in his life. Admittedly, Dr. Guernsey was ill-prepared for this task. He tried everything he could think of. He employed every spiritual resource, approach and method that he knew about, read about or was encouraged to try by people from Christian liturgical traditions other than his own. Nothing worked.

Finally, one day sitting in his office with John, with tears streaming down his face, Dr. Guernsey told him he was sorry that he couldn't help him. He concluded by saying, "John, all I know is that I love you."

At this, John leaped out of his chair, ran to the window of his office, threw it open and let out a blood-curdling scream. Then he fell limp on the floor—completely free of any demonic presence in his life.

As Dr. Guernsey concluded his story of John's deliverance from demonic oppression, he expressed concern that few U.S. pastors, therapists and missionaries are prepared to confront the demonic powers that oppress and twist human behavior. As a result of his experience with John, he was now convinced that demons do exist and that people can be freed from physical, emotional and spiritual bondage to live new and productive lives.

The existence of demons and their influence on human beings is a topic hotly debated among American Christians. Our rational Western worldview makes it difficult for us to believe in the supernatural; therefore we tend to demythologize and limit spiritual forces to the realm of material phenomena that can be explained, understood and controlled. We often ignore, dismiss or rationalize the existence of angels, demons, and unseen powers and principalities.

Dietrich Bonhoeffer, the Lutheran minister who stood up to the tyranny of Nazi Germany, wrote, "How can one close one's eyes at the fact that the demons themselves have taken over rule of the world, that it is the powers of darkness who have here made an awful conspiracy?"[1] The apostle Paul makes it explicitly clear that "our struggle is not against enemies of blood and flesh, but against the rulers, against the authorities, against the cosmic powers of this present darkness, against the spiritual forces of evil in the heavenly places" (Ephesians 6:12). According to Paul, principalities and powers are the personalities and forces that dominate our lives and our world. These personalities and forces are visible and invisible, earthly and heavenly. They include human rulers, large world structures, angelic beings like Michael and demonic beings like Satan. Appendix 3 in this book gives a crucial biblical basis for Brenda and Rick's understanding of the principalities and powers if you want to explore more deeply.

These unseen powers and principalities seem to reveal themselves through human beings and the institutions we create. "What we call the state, the economy, the media, ideology—these are their instruments."[2] The powers and principalities use these instruments to influence human behavior, events and structures to propagate social myths that have immense power and control in our lives.

This demonic ability to influence human behavior and infiltrate human systems can be seen in all its destructive power in the sin of personal and institutional racism. In 1963 civil rights activist and lawyer William Stringfellow stunned delegates at the first National Conference on Religion and Race in Chicago by unmasking these powers and principalities in a speech he gave on racism in America. He said:

> The monstrous American heresy is in thinking that the whole drama of history takes place between God and humanity. But the truth, biblically and theologically and empirically, is quite otherwise: The drama of this history takes place amongst God and humanity and the principalities and powers, the great institutions and ideologies active in the world. It is the corruption and shallowness of humanism, which beguiles Jew or Christian into believing that human beings are masters of institution or ideology. . . . Racism is not an evil in human hearts and minds; it is a principality, a demonic power, a representative image, an embodiment of death, over which human beings have little or no control, but which works its awful influence in their lives.[3]

As we come to the fourth step of the spiritual transformation model of ethnic healing and racial justice, it is important to note that until now we have largely kept our focus off the demonic dimensions of racism. Until now we have not engaged directly with principalities and powers. Instead, we have focused our attention on God in worship, on our ethnic identity, and on our sin in its enslaving power. Focusing first in these directions has been a very deliberate decision. We are convinced that an unhealthy focus on the demonic dimension of racism does more harm than good. If we try to take on these forces and cast them out in nonbiblical or extrabiblical ways, as some people teach, we put ourselves at risk. We call unnecessary attention to ourselves. Powerful forces are good at crushing people. Casting out large forces and demonic beings throws down a gauntlet, issuing a challenge that is very difficult to support from Scripture and that often results in confusion and chaos.

Since we began by aligning our souls aright with God, we can now name, unmask and renounce the false gods related to racism and ethnocentrism. These forces and past idolatries have controlled and bound us. However, the good news is that just as the cross of Christ brings forgiveness of sin, it also brings freedom from the principalities and powers.

So what is the biblical way to encounter and engage with larger forces and demonic personalities? In this chapter we want to explore a way of encounter and engagement based on the model of Jesus recorded in the Synoptic Gospels, especially Matthew. But before we do, we can't emphasize enough that the first three stages of our model set in place the strength, perspective and attitude to engage demonic principalities and powers in a healthy, humble, effectual way.

NAMING THE DEMONIC POWERS BEHIND RACISM

We are convinced that there are demonic forces—supernatural entities—at work behind the scenes that perpetuate the evils of racism, ethnic cleansing and tribalism around the world. We believe that one of the demons at work in racial and ethnic hatred is the spirit of pride. This spirit, also referred to as the spirit of the empire, leads to militaristic aggression, technological control and genocide and has caused untold human suffering, mass destruction and oppression for centuries. The work of this spirit can be seen in the worldwide conquests of the British empire, in the dominance of the Spanish empire in Latin America, in the evil system of apartheid in South Africa, and in systems of slavery in North and South America and elsewhere in the world.

The spirit of pride or the spirit of the empire drives people to conquer and vanquish others based on the evil, insidious ideology of racial and ethnic superiority. This supernatural entity refuses to submit to God and produces a human arrogance that attempts to make God and others in one's own image. Many historians have pointed out how evil Adolf Hitler was. There seems to have been a demonic power working through his personality with unusual intensity. At the heart of the evil of the Nazi regime was Hitler's doctrine of Aryan—racial German—supremacy. This doctrine fostered hatred, scapegoating, and attacks on all people and all things Semitic. Racism and genocide are two of the distinguishing indicators of the rule of Satan in our world.

Rick Joyner, an author who is a prophetic voice in our day, agrees that racism is deeply rooted in the spirit of pride: "There is possibly no pride greater than the belief that God is just like us!"[4] This belief operates at a level of assumptions that are often unconscious. However, its outworking has caused violence, hatred and disdain for people of certain racial and ethnic groups, distorting human relationships and fostering a deadly, pervasive sense of isolation and apathy. Racism and ethnocentrism—the exalting of our own ethnic identity and cultural characteristics—and the accompanying rationale of inferiority of other ethnic groups and people have been one of the most destructive forces in world history. The divide-and-conquer tactic of the enemy of our souls has left scars on the souls of oppressed and oppressor alike.

We only have to rehearse the history of Asian Americans, Latinos, African Americans and Native Americans to see this very evil spirit at work. Asians were first brought to the United States to provide cheap labor for mining and building railroads on the West Coast. When their labor was no longer needed, Asians—especially Chinese—were excluded from jobs and citizenship, prevented from bringing their wives and families to join them, and even murdered during race riots in the nineteenth century. During World War II, Japanese people were interned in prison camps, losing their homes, jobs and families as a result of racial profiling. Today, there are approximately twenty-nine Asian groups in the United States; however, they are all aggregated into one category, thus enabling myths and stereotypes about Asian Americans to flourish.

Native American people were systematically moved or killed as their land was stolen from them and given to people of European descent. The deadly effects of this systematic slaughter of a people are still evident in the substandard living conditions on reservations in America today.

Latino people have also had lands and livelihoods taken away from them. The Mexican American War was fought to gain land for the United States at a time when Mexico was vulnerable to such a conquest. The destabilizing effects of this subjugation are still evident in the abject poverty suffered in many parts of Mexico today.

Then there is the sobering history of African Americans—the only people group brought to the United States against their will. These people were used like animals to provide free labor for European Americans and were systematically stigmatized as inferior to justify their slavery, rape, mutilation and murder.

We believe that these injustices and inequalities are evidence of the works of the powers and principalities that seek to kill, steal and destroy human life. We don't have to look far to see these forces at work in our world today. The spirit of mammon is another spiritual power in our world today that is closely tied to the spirit of pride. It propagates the lie that money is more important than human life. The love of money and the quest for economic and material wealth were often—and still are—at the root of slavery and human subjugation. Where the spirit of mammon is operating, human beings are objectified and reduced to commodities, property that can be bought or sold.

The spirit of fear is another spiritual power behind racism and division we experience in our world today. This spirit propagates the xenophobia—hatred of strangers or foreigners—that is prevalent in our world. Blind fear of anything or anyone different from one's own people group has produced heightened suspicion, hostility and distrust between people from diverse racial and ethnic backgrounds. The spirit of fear is at the root of racially motivated hate crimes, unjust immigration laws and racial profiling practices that have destroyed lives and discriminated against people in attempts to protect ourselves from the other.

The spirit of pride and the spirit of the empire can also be seen whenever we start to feel a sense of manifest destiny to save the world and police all the bad guys. It is true that governments are called to protect their people and to trade with their neighbors; however, when we cross the line of being one nation among many and start to think of ourselves as the chosen nation, the best nation and the Big Brother of all other nations, we have fallen into self-worship and idolatry. So the spirits of pride and empire building, of mammon and of fear influence nations through ethnocentric systems, beliefs and practices from which we must be freed.

FREEDOM FROM THE POWERS AND PRINCIPALITIES

If we want to fulfill our true identity as the church, we must reclaim our authority to unmask, denounce and disarm the spiritual powers that war against Christ and his kingdom. This will require that we engage the personal, social and spiritual dimensions of racism. We expose the schemes of the powers and the principalities by living counterculturally, coming against them in prayer and proclaiming Christ's victory over them through the power of the gospel.

To aid us in this process, William Stringfellow helpfully suggests that the idolatry of nations and their particular principalities and powers can be analyzed by looking at the following three dimensions of idolatry:

1. *Ideologies* that reinforce a sense of chosenness and specialness and right to dominate others.

2. *Institutions* that reinforce a sense of chosenness and specialness and right to dominate others, and

3. *Images* that reinforce a sense of chosenness and specialness and right to dominate others.[5]

These three dimensions of idolatry can be seen in the life of the children of Israel in the Old Testament. For Israel, the *ideology* was a theology of chosenness that was used to keep some people in and at the top and other people down and out. All self-justifying ideologies work in this way: strengths, advantages and good fortune become the rationale for keeping power, grasping privilege, and excluding the weak and the foe from blessing. The *institution* was the temple, which became a place of exclusion. No wonder Jesus was incensed at the temple practices that kept Gentiles, women, the poor, the blind and the lame from worshiping God. The temple had become the symbol of Jewish male supremacy. The *image* was the Torah, which was symbolized by the phylacteries the Pharisees wore and the scrolls read in the synagogues. The Torah (Genesis through Deuteronomy) was intended to teach all people to love God and others, but it became a means of marginalizing or excluding women, Gentiles, the poor, the lame, lepers and the blind from God's covenant community.

Jesus confronted his nation's idolatry and ideology and chose freedom, but in the end it was at the cost of his life. It is very costly to confront any nation's ideology and idolatry, to choose freedom for yourself and to invite others into freedom. Jesus chose this path, and it led to the cross.

Jesus also pursued lost sheep everywhere in Israel. He told them the good news: now the poor, the mourners, the persecuted, the really needy and the deeply sinned against of Israel were receiving God's kingdom, while the rich, powerful and religious were being judged. He discerned the idolatry of his nation, and he discerned and exposed its impact on the poor, marginalized and excluded within Israel. And when he saw who the system of chosenness and dominance excluded and marginalized, that was who he lovingly sought to reach.

The American civil rights movement likewise involved discerning and exposing the impact of national ideology and idolatry on the poor and marginalized. Defenseless black people being hosed and beaten awakened the conscience of a nation. We saw the impact of Jim Crow and the theories of white supremacy and black inferiority in the abuse of the poor. Jesus, like Martin Luther King Jr., did not just go around talking about the presence and power of evil and the principalities and powers. He exposed the evil at the heart of society by choosing, liberating and giving courage to those who had been most victimized in his nation. Jesus' ministry was a positive ministry of restoring God's rule to the poor, the lost and the left behind, and in so doing he exposed the powers and principalities that were at work in his day.

After Jesus died and rose, it was the apostles, and now we in the church, who were and are the suffering servants carrying that message and ministry to the nations. Each nation has its own gods, ideologies, institutions and images that are to be named and confronted. And in each nation, the least and the lost and beaten down must be loved and reached and invited into the kingdom community.

In the West we can fool ourselves into thinking that if we understand a problem, we have solved the problem. We believe that knowledge is power, and so when we articulate a brilliant critique we think we have gained the victory. But critique is not enough. Though truth makes freedom possible, it is only love for the least and the lost that brings the kingdom of God near. Only love has power to cast out fear. And behind the system of dominance and superiority there is immense fear—on both sides of any conflict.

The principalities and powers have a lot invested in the system of pride, dominance, rage and revenge that drives our world. Principalities and powers love the never-ending cycle of sin and counter-sin, of dominance and revenge. They are fighting like hell to keep us a divided human race, battling each other and worshiping them. Their power is wrapped up in the enslaving power of sin.

And so their power is broken as we enter into genuine forgiveness and authentic reconciliation. When we confess our sins of pride and revenge, we unmask the principalities and powers and their claim to enslave us. We expose the spirit of pride and empire building when we confess it as the sin that it is and turn from it toward the cross. We expose the spirit of fear and hatred of the other when we confess it for the sin that it is and turn toward the cross. These powers in the world are exposed and defanged. They lose their right to rule us.

So Jesus calls us to make disciples, not just of individuals but even of people groups and nations: "All authority in heaven and earth has been given to me. Now, let's go on to all the other nations of the earth. You will make disciples of the *nations* (not just individuals), baptizing in the name of the Father, Son and Holy Spirit, and teaching them to obey all that I have commanded you. And remember (in this task of discipling the nations), I am with you always, to the end of the age" (see Matthew 28:18-20).

It is our conviction that the gospel message in the New Testament is always proclaimed in light of the principalities and powers that enslave and divide people. When a person converts to Jesus Christ, it is always a personal *and* social act—a radical switch of allegiances between kingdoms. These kingdoms are spiritual, institutional, corporate, economic and personal. They are heavenly and earthly, visible and invisible. In other words, the gospel proclaims not only forgiveness of personal sins but repentance from and renunciation of the rulers of this present darkness and their demonic influence over our lives and over nations.

ENGAGING THE PRINCIPALITIES AND POWERS

As we follow the example of Jesus, we are given a pattern for engaging and denouncing principalities and powers in our own life and ministry.

Disciple nations (ethnic groups). In his ministry Jesus did not just address, confront and mentor individuals. Jesus addressed, confronted and discipled a whole nation, the nation of Israel. *We too are called to disciple nations, not just individuals.* As we go to the ends of the earth, we are to make disciples of the nations—the peoples or ethnic groups—baptizing them in the name of the Father, Son and Holy Spirit and teaching them to obey all that Jesus taught. A crucial part of discipling a nation and the individuals who are part of that nation is to expose the principalities and powers that dominate that nation.

We will never discern the principalities and powers that distort and dehumanize our ethnic group or nation unless we begin to ask for discernment. Many of us have never thought about the ethnocentrism of our own ethnic group or nation. Many of us have never unpacked those corporate issues. But those issues are crucial. Until we identify and renounce our corporate sins and idolatry, those things will enslave and rule us as a people. To faithfully preach the·gospel, we need to know how the gospel addresses us not just as individuals but also as a people. Too often the principalities and powers have conspired to keep us ignorant of their control. They love it when we preach a gospel that affects only individuals. This enables them to keep their power.

We've seen it again and again. Churches offer individuals forgiveness but remain enslaved to a lifestyle of militarism or materialism or racism. Such a gospel can actually reinforce the enslaving lifestyle and the rule of principalities and powers. That's really the point of Michael Emerson and Christian Smith's *Divided by Faith*. Our individualistic gospel has left the powers of racism and ethnocentrism unaffected. We the church are as divided and racially isolated as every other institution in our society, and maybe more so. That's why critics of the church enjoy pointing out that 11:00 a.m. on Sundays is the most segregated hour of the week in America.

As long as our idolatries remain unexposed and unconfronted and our ethnocentrism remains hidden, racial reconciliation is not really possible or authentic. So we must recover the call to make disciples of nations, peoples and ethnic groups. We must also recover the mandate to discern and turn away from our corporate sins and idolatries—especially ethnocentric ideologies of chosenness.

Engage the principalities and powers. In pursuit of this ministry of kingdom realization, Jesus engaged with the principalities and powers over Israel. Those principalities and powers included the ideology of chosenness, the institution of the temple, the image of Torah and the personality behind it all, Satan. We too are called to discern the principalities and powers over our nation and ethnic group, to discern their subtle strategy, to reject it and them, and to embrace the supremacy and victory of God in our own lives.

Here are some good questions we can ruminate on in a place of prayer and solitude, asking the Spirit to lead us into greater discernment of the powers and principalities that influence our racial or ethnic group.

1. What is our people's particular theory of specialness or chosenness?

2. What institutions especially support that theory?

3. What images in our common life symbolize the main things that we worship about ourselves? (The dollar, the bomb, the presidential seal and the flag all come to mind for the United States, for example.)

4. What people are excluded or looked upon as inferior as a result of our theory of our specialness?

5. What human personality and demonic presence might lie behind our theory of our specialness? What false gods might our fathers and mothers have worshiped?

A Korean American woman worked through some of these questions and was eventually able to renounce the gods that her ancestors worshiped. She came to Rick for prayer and counsel because she had been having demonic dreams. After talking to her family, she realized that these dreams were very similar to dreams her mother had at the same point in her life. She learned that in the past Korean people had turned to shamanistic practices to seek healing and guidance (shamanistic practices include attempts to influence spirits that cause sickness). Although this practice was commonplace, when some Koreans become followers of Jesus Christ few of them are taught to renounce the gods of their fathers and mothers. As a result, these demonic cultural influences can erupt at various points until they are identified, named and renounced. This young woman learned that she needed to speak aloud a renunciation of the shamanistic practices that had been carried out by her ancestors. When she did so, she was freed from the demonic dreams that had been plaguing her.

Freedom from the gods of our ancestors can sometimes be gained only as we identify the gods of past generations and declare our freedom in Christ from them. Otherwise, these gods and the false worship that was given to them can affect children in our family line for generations to come.

For all of us, the path of freedom begins with identifying the sin and idolatry, naming it and renouncing our idol. In this case we need to confess our ethnocentrism, not just vaguely but specifically. *We have thought that our culture and our people are at the center. We have thought that God especially chooses us.* We have had different rationales. For white Americans, it has been our success, our technology and our Christian roots. But for other people, the sense of superiority and destiny has been tied to other things. Maybe it is our achievements or our suffering or our roots. Whatever it is, we need to identify it and turn away from it toward God.

Then we renounce all of our devotion to any false gods, any demonic personalities—that includes Satan, but it may also include the gods that our ancestors worshiped. To do this we need to carry out practical and symbolic acts of freedom from our ethnocentrism and idolatry. We can place symbols of our superiority—perhaps a computer, a dollar, a diploma or a characteristic form of dress—on the altar and proclaim that these things are called to serve God and people and not to rule over us.

Above all, we can worship together and celebrate our unity. Acts of reconciliation and unity are powerful proclamations to the principalities and powers related to ethnocentrism that their divisive rule is over and done (see Ephesians 3:6, 10). Communion together, worship together, prayer together, standing for Christ together is the most radical act of freedom from the principalities and powers that we can pursue.

Find and proclaim freedom to lost people in our nation. Out of his freedom from the principalities and powers, Jesus pursued a ministry that made the kingdom of God available to every lost sheep/person in Israel, especially those most victimized by the principalities and powers. Jesus then backed up his ministry with his death, and God vindicated his victory by raising Jesus from the dead and making his victory through the cross available to all the nations of the earth. We too are called to use our freedom to make the kingdom of God available to every lost person in our nation or ethnic group. And we too are called to pay the price of confrontation with evil, trusting in God's vindication!

There are always marginalized people whom no one is reaching because they are somehow seen as inferior and excluded. We are called to reach them and invite them into the full experience of the kingdom of God. We are also called to name those things about ourselves that exclude and alienate people from inclusion in God's kingdom. Often our stereotypes and fears keep us isolated and unaware of the needs of people who aren't like us. Every church or ministry needs to be reaching out to those whom we might tend to exclude or judge or fear. The good news of the kingdom finds its richest, deepest and most powerful expression as we seek the alienated and excluded.

What's more, identifying with people unlike us and taking initia-

tive to reach out to them brings us face to face with our own stereotypes, prejudices and ethnocentrism. As we face our proud and judgmental nature, we can confess it before God and others. In fact right
now we might well ask ourselves a few incisive questions:

• How do we respond to the poor?

• Does our faith free us to be reconciled across racial and cultural
  boundaries?

• How vibrant and explosive is the gospel of the kingdom in our
  midst? Are churches being planted?

• Do we have wisdom to listen to other peoples about whether or
  not to go to war?

• Do we have courage to face our militarism, our racist history, our
  materialism and greed?

Our answers to these questions will alert us to whether or not we
are proclaiming through our life, words and deeds the message of
Jesus that will heal people and nations.

WHEN THE PRINCIPALITIES AND POWERS PERSECUTE US

Possibly the most courageous speech Rev. Dr. Martin Luther King Jr.
ever gave was a sermon at Riverside Church in New York, where he
made a connection between the Vietnam War and civil rights. He saw
and said that the two principalities of racism and militarism were related and in league with one another. The prejudice and economic
self-absorption that led America to a war in Vietnam had also led
America to placate blacks and other minorities in this country without
really pursuing justice. King confronted these twin principalities,
knowing that the cause of equality and civil rights would be attacked

but his integrity and the integrity of the gospel would be vindicated. As he wrote much earlier in his "Letter from Birmingham Jail": "Injustice anywhere is a threat to justice everywhere. We are caught in an inescapable network of mutuality, tied to a single garment of destiny."[6]

Dr. King deeply believed that this was true. He was focused on not just the fate of his own people but the fate of all people. He proclaimed God's kingdom at Riverside Church, and he paid a great price to do so. Surveillance, wiretaps and threats were increased all the more after he took this stand against the war. Friends and enemies alike criticized and rejected him.

When we are honest about the principalities and powers of militarism, racism and materialism and about our fear and pride, we will find that our audience will get smaller. An example of this is what happened to the Promise Keepers movement after founder Bill McCartney made racial and ethnic reconciliation one of its seven promises for men and for the church in our day—to the surprise, shock and even resistance of many conservative evangelical people. Here is his description of his experience of challenging church people to work for racial reconciliation among God's people: "Always when I finished there was no response—nothing. No applause. No smiles. Everyone looked crestfallen. In city after city, in church after church, it was the same story—wild enthusiasm while I was being introduced, followed by a morguelike chill as I stepped away from the microphone."[7]

To this day, the racial reconciliation message remains a highly charged element of Promise Keepers' ministry. It is our belief that the commitment to racial reconciliation was a major factor in the significant falloff in Promise Keepers attendance. It is simply a hard teaching for many.

Jesus calls us to joy when we experience rejection and criticism, for we have been counted worthy to suffer with him (Matthew 5:11-12). Often God uses our weakness more than our strength to expose evil. As theologian Marva Dawn rightly observes:

> Even as Christ accomplished victory through weakness, suffering and death, so the Lord accomplishes witness to the world through weakness. God has more need of our weakness than of our strength. Just as the powers overstep their bounds and become gods, so our power becomes a rival to God. By our union with Christ in the power of the Spirit in our weaknesses, we display God's glory.[8]

How do we find and choose joy in those times? We need one another to restore joy. Bridge people need other bridge people. Gatherings of bridge people can restore joy, strengthen resolve and sharpen our focus. So in addition to bridge people we need bridge *groups*.

Rick was part of such a small group for many years with his former pastor and mentor Bill Leslie. Bill, who was a pioneer in urban ministry and had founded LaSalle Street Church in Chicago, knew firsthand the loneliness and persecution that one faces when pursuing racial healing and justice. He created this group for emerging young leaders like Rick, and to this day Rick feels it was one of the few places he could be at home.

Maybe you could start such a group. Or maybe there is an older bridge person you respect; you could go to this person, ask for mentoring and encourage him or her to draw in others with you. Attending conferences such as those sponsored by the Christian Community Development Association is another way to restore your soul in the presence of like-minded people. Brenda is a frequent speaker at such conferences, and in these gatherings she finds joy, perspective, encouragement and supportive fellowship.

God calls us to boldness in confronting the principalities and powers. God also calls us to joy when we experience rejection, criticism and loneliness. For that work of restoration and healing, we need one another. We need each other to help us keep perspective and not take ourselves too seriously.

As surprising as it may sound, in the fight for ethnic healing and racial justice against the powers and the principalities, we must learn to laugh. We need the humility and holy laughter exhibited in the life of Francis of Assisi, the friar who confronted the materialism and church corruption of his day. He saw himself as a holy fool. He could laugh at himself and see his own foibles and follies with clarity. In so doing, he was able to keep his heart from despairing and increased his longevity in ministry.

RENOUNCING THE POWERS

Now that we have clarified scriptural principles for engaging the powers and principalities that wage war against the healing of people and the healing of nations, we invite you to renounce these ideologies, forces and spirits and become free of them by speaking aloud the baptismal vows of the early church.

Do you renounce Satan and all the spiritual forces of wickedness that rebel against God?

I renounce them.

Do you renounce the evil powers of this world, which corrupt and destroy the creatures of God?

I renounce them.

Do you renounce all sinful desires that draw you from the love of God?

I renounce them.

Do you turn to Jesus Christ and accept him as your Savior?

I do.

Do you put your whole trust in his grace and love?

I do.

Do you promise to follow and obey him as your Lord?

I do.[9]

Lord, we thank you for your call to be free from the influence and control of the principalities and powers. We thank you for the ability to discern them and renounce them so that we may come into greater freedom in our lives and in the church. We sense your holy call to recover vital dimensions of the gospel that have been lost to us. We confess that we have been ignorant of the principalities and powers. We have not discerned their corporate and institutional expressions amongst us. So now, Lord, we repent, and we invite your Holy Spirit to come and teach us to discern. We want our discernment to be filled with your presence. We embrace your way of humility that produces strength in weakness to defeat the very powers of hell. Thank you, Lord. We submit ourselves to your lordship afresh. Amen.

9

ONGOING PARTNERSHIPS

When Rick was a new InterVarsity staff worker in Madison, Wisconsin, an African American brother named Ron Meyers prayed a prayer for him that we now jokingly refer to as "the Ignorant White Brother Prayer." Ron said, "I pray for my ignorant white brother. He doesn't know, Lord. He doesn't understand how much his ignorance and apathy hurt me. And he doesn't even know that he doesn't know! O God, open his eyes. Help my brother. He wants to help. He just doesn't know how, because he knows so little about me and my life and the life of black people in America. God help him."

Once worlds apart in their cultural backgrounds and understanding of racial reconciliation, Rick and Dr. Ronald V. Meyers Sr., the "Delta Doctor," are great friends today. Although they live in two different states, they have maintained contact over the years, supported each other's ministries, and taught on racial reconciliation and justice together. How did this change take place? It occurred through an on-going partnership that began when Rick had just graduated from college and made a conscious decision to submit himself to Ron's leadership by serving on his ministry team. Through this ongoing collaborative relationship Rick learned more about what he didn't know. He learned about black history, the plight of black people in America, economic and racial injustice, and how to do urban ministry by serving with the people.

It was not an easy process, and there were many times when both men wanted to give up on this difficult, challenging relationship. However, the turning point came when Ron asked Rick a life-changing question after they had weathered a particularly thorny struggle. He said, "Rick, do you know to the bottom of your heart that I really love you and that I'm committed to you and that I'm really thankful God brought us together?"

The question came as a shock to Rick, because until then he had often felt judged, misunderstood and sometimes even used by Ron. The sincerity and vulnerability of Ron's question fostered a greater level of honesty between a white boy from the Midwest and a black man from the South. It began a process of really getting to know and trust each other, and this process gradually produced a genuine partnership that has lasted for years.

THE PROBLEM OF ISOLATION

Rick's condition when he began is the condition in which most of us begin: ignorant, isolated and alienated from people who are unlike us. We are strangers who communicate differently, have different cultures, eat different foods, enjoy different music and see the world from different points of view. We are socialized to label these differences as inferior or superior, right or wrong, normal or abnormal, safe or dangerous, good or bad. We alienate ourselves from people who are unlike us and develop an aversion to them based on our prejudices, stereotypes and fears. This cultural isolation and alienation breeds the xenophobia that is at the core of racism and ethnocentrism. People who stay isolated in this posture of fear often use their power and influence to preserve their culture and familiar way of life. In so doing they consciously or unconsciously discriminate and limit the life choices and opportunities of people from other racial and ethnic backgrounds. This use of power is demonstrated in how we vote, where we live, shop, attend church and send our children to school, and whom we choose to hire or recommend for a job. Such decisions are made in an attempt to preserve our way of life and protect the culture that we perceive to be superior.

As Christians, we have been entrusted with the ministry of reconciliation and called to live a countercultural lifestyle that has the potential to inspire hope in people all around the world. Barbara Williams Skinner, a well-known leader and advocate in the international movement for peace and reconciliation, makes a similar point. She says that Christians in the United States have been given a unique opportunity and responsibility: "As the world's most powerful nation, efforts in America toward healing Black-White racial tension will have a tremendous impact on ending the alienation with Latinos, Asians, Native Americans in this nation and among people experiencing fractured relationships around the world."[1]

MOVING INTO COMMUNITY

In order for potential reconcilers to move from ignorance and isolation into a lifestyle of racial and ethnic reconciliation, they must develop ongoing partnerships that support their desire and commitment to be people God can use in the healing of people and nations. It is critical that people begin to live out what they believe about racial and ethnic reconciliation in their daily life, choice of friends, place of worship, and economic and political decisions. These behaviors, exercised consistently over an extended period of time, are what establish racial and ethnic reconciliation as an authentic core value in the life of a person or group. Ongoing partnerships create a context in which trust is developed—a level of trust that allows people to challenge and support each other on tough issues regarding the use of their influence to promote justice and equality for all people. Together, as a community of faith, they make a commitment to extend themselves into the world to create structures and systems that promote peace, justice and reconciliation for people of every nationality.

Within a sustaining community people who desire to be reconcilers learn from each other and become aware of the things they do not know. Through ongoing partnerships they develop awareness of the social conditions around them. In order to be relevant in this generation, this awareness must go beyond personal relationships to include institutional, social and global levels. Lack of awareness and exposure to social and global issues leads to ignorance and individualism, and these give rise in turn to racism and unhealthy patriotism. Therefore a commitment to grow in awareness is a primary step in the process of becoming an ambassador for racial and ethnic reconciliation who can be used to heal people and nations.

Often the needed awareness grows when people are immersed in another culture. Mission trips can be immensely transforming, as we leave the culture in which we are part of a majority to experience life from other people's viewpoints. This experience can give us perspective on our culture, our temperament, our need to control our life, our sources of security, and our status and privilege in our society. The discipline of "fasting" from being a majority person in our culture may be the single most transforming step we can take in becoming reconcilers.

With new awareness, the emerging reconciler can begin to develop a new reference group of people with whom to relate and identify. This new group is best composed of people from different racial and ethnic backgrounds who have very little in common on the surface but who share a desire to develop genuine understanding of and appreciation for others. As the members of this diverse group engage with each other—sharing their stories and getting to know each other by being honest and vulnerable—empathy and bond begin to form between them.

During this process, some of the automatic assumptions, perceptions and stereotypes people have held about others are challenged and changed. It's all too easy to enter a group of strangers and make prejudgments about them before getting to know them as people. On one occasion Brenda helped to facilitate an ethnic diversity training session for a group of white male managers in Colorado. As she entered the room and saw a group of well-dressed white men, she immediately assumed that she had them pretty well figured out. As the training progressed and each man began to share his story, though, it became apparent that these men were radically different from each other. One man explained that racial reconciliation was extremely important to him because his oldest son is Korean and struggles with his ethnic identity. He later revealed that he had six children, all adopted, who have special needs and are from different racial and ethnic backgrounds. Brenda and some of his other colleagues had never heard this before; as a result of the diversity training workshop they all grew in appreciation and respect for this man.

This experience taught Brenda a very valuable lesson. She now knows firsthand the truth of the old adage "You can't judge a book by its cover." And telling stories is a powerful way for people to reveal themselves and give others the opportunity to see who they really are—what is inside the book.

In addition to sharing our story with others, a crucial step in the identification process is to learn from leaders of a different race and ethnicity by submitting ourselves to their leadership. As recounted in the opening story of this chapter, Rick joined a ministry to African Americans and committed himself to serving under an African American leader. Serving under those of a different ethnicity or race is an especially crucial discipline for white Americans today. Often whites have failed to notice the many assumptions and perceptions that give them power and leverage wherever they go. When whites submit to the leadership of people of color, opportunities to identify, examine and confront their distorted views and prideful attitudes will emerge in the context of loving, ongoing partnership.

It was a humbling experience, but Rick had to receive the "ignorant white brother" prayer. In the beginning of his campus ministry Rick was actually pretty useless in reaching out to black students. He also felt powerless when Ron and Stan, the African American leaders, expected him to find financial and material resources for the ministry.

Rick had to take his frustrations and sense of uselessness to God.

In retrospect, this was a very good thing for Rick to grapple with. In the work for justice and reconciliation, often the people of color have to carry most of the disappointment, frustration and hurt. Through all those hard experiences Rick learned to identify with hurting people and the frustrations experienced by people of color, and this equipped him for relating differently in a multiethnic world. The discipline of submission, then, is particularly useful for helping people from the majority culture to experience life from the perspective of people of color.

TOSS OUT THE SCRIPT

In addition to this call to submission, we want to passionately call people to engage reconciliation in ways that get beyond the "script." There is a script for the racial reconciliation process that is helpful in some ways but destructive in others. When Rick almost crashed and burned in the quest for racial and ethnic reconciliation, he discovered that white people have a certain scripted role in that struggle. It seems that they are expected to (1) repent of their racism and (2) work behind the scenes to raise money and open organizational doors so people of color can lead. There are good things about this script, but it can be very limiting. Specifically, Rick was not very good at working behind the scenes to raise money, manage people and open organizational doors for people of color. Only later did he realize that a major factor in his failure and near burnout had been his unquestioning submission to the script. He tried hard, but the script didn't fit his gifts, capabilities and calling. As a result, Rick ended up feeling that he had nothing left to offer in the struggle for ethnic and racial reconciliation.

White people like Rick need to realize that when they get involved in racial reconciliation, too often they want to take over, write the books and run the show. They need to remain very responsive to the leadership and insight of people of color. But they certainly have more to give than their money! Rick needed to become free to contribute to racial reconciliation and justice according to his gifts and calling.

People of color also have a script. They are expected to represent their whole race, speak out for justice and focus their life on justice for their community and their people. There are many good things about this script as well, but it can also be very limiting. Too many people of color have left their community and never looked back to help others. Still, people of color are much more than just their ethnic background.

We all are called to learn from the scripts we have been given. But now more than ever, we must go beyond those scripts into authentic relationship and genuine partnership. The spiritual transformation model helps us live in newfound freedom and vision for a new stage of partnership. We are thankful to God for the freedom and power that have come as we have chosen to go beyond the script and partner with each other in new ways, according to our particular gifts and the contribution each of us can make.

The process of identifying with others allows people to see themselves as unique individuals, not just as members of a particular racial or ethnic group. This is the beginning of forming a new identity and moving beyond categories and stereotypes. Through ongoing engagement with those who are racially and ethnically different, people are helped to see themselves as more than they or society thought they were. They are given a vision of who they can be as people committed to peace, justice and reconciliation. They are able to align themselves with others who are also learning and growing in racial and ethnic reconciliation. This is a vital component of healthy, ongoing partnerships and is crucial to the reconciliation process.

DEVELOPING NEW SKILLS

In addition to forming a new identity in the context of a sustaining community, people seeking to participate in the ministry of racial and ethnic reconciliation need to develop particular skills. In *Divided by Faith* sociologists Michael Emerson and Christian Smith identify a "lack of serious thinking" as a major obstacle for evangelical Christians in racial reconciliation:

> With few exceptions, evangelicals lack serious thinking on [race relations in America]. Rather than integrate their faith with knowledge of race relations, inequality, and American society, they generally allow their cultural constructions to shape one-dimensional assessments and solutions to multidimensional problems. This will not do. The first new step evangelicals might consider, therefore, is engaging in more serious reflection on race-relations issues, in dialogue with educated others.[2]

They go on to quote N. K. Clifford, who argues, "The Evangelical Protestant mind has never relished complexity. Indeed its crusading genius, whether in religion or politics, has always tended toward an oversimplification of the issues and the substitution of inspiration and zeal for critical analysis and serious reflection."[3] Thus we believe that effective ongoing partnerships must be committed to gathering information and to thinking critically about it in order to facilitate racial and ethnic reconciliation.

To effectively engage in ethnic diversity and reconciliation, Christians must develop improved information gathering and critical thinking skills in order to become better educated on the causes of crosscultural conflicts. This will require that people go beyond the confines of traditional thinking and question the messages they have received from their ethnic group or family of origin. They must seek out alternative information sources that provide more complete and accurate pictures of the problems than are generally available through the conventional news media. Having gathered the information, they must then analyze it to determine its validity, relevance and potential meaning.

Second, potential reconcilers must develop effective intercultural communication skills. An ability to communicate with clarity is essential for developing mutual understanding, greater crosscultural awareness and deeper appreciation for people from different racial and ethnic backgrounds. In the reconciliation process people must be given the opportunity to voice their thoughts and concerns without fear of interruption or reprimand. This will require that other members of the group listen empathically, without judgment or argument. Communicating effectively is absolutely essential to encourage honest dialogue across racial, ethnic and cultural differences.

For healthy dialogue about racial and ethnic issues to be facilitated, these communication skills must be exercised in the context of a loving multiethnic group or community. This means that ongoing partnerships must also develop community-building skills. Psychologist M. Scott Peck explores such skills in his seminal book on peace-making, *The Different Drum: Community Making and Peace.*[4] He identifies four stages necessary for building authentic community: pseudo-community, chaos, emptying and community. In the *pseudo-community* stage people engage at a cordial but superficial level. This involves the type of social interaction most people experience daily with coworkers and casual acquaintances. The stage that follows is aptly named *chaos,* for Peck suggests that people must experience conflict and loss of control if they are to move beyond superficiality to true community. This crucial turning point in any group's development comes when people take the risk to recognize and express their differences. The third stage is called *emptying* because people must empty themselves of the need to change, persuade or convince others in the group to adopt their point of view. Instead, as members become vulnerable and transparent, the group moves through conflict to a place of mutual understanding and respect. This leads to the final stage, *community.* In this stage people reveal their true selves, are accepted for who they are, and experience the personal transformation and healing that occur only in such an affirming and accepting environment. The skills involved in navigating these stages are crucial to building trust and promoting intercultural relationships across racial and ethnic lines.

Since chaos is inevitable in the community-building process, problem-solving and conflict resolution skills are also vital. Hearing another's concerns without defending, justifying or protecting oneself is the essence of nondefensive listening. Openness and adaptability are required for promoting compromise and negotiating a win-win solution to conflict whenever possible. In addition, those involved in reconciliation efforts must be able to work with others to accurately define and assess the scope of a problem from different perspectives. Those attempting reconciliation must have clarity to assess joint resources and be able to devise a plan, strategy and course of action for solving problems and resolving conflict.

Finally, because our call to racial and ethnic reconciliation is rooted in a biblical mandate, Christians must be committed to reading Scripture with new openness and willingness to learn. This will require the inductive learning skills of observation, interpretation and application. Rather than accepting the traditional messages about the Bible's teachings on race, culture and ethnicity, inductive learners study and discover biblical truth for themselves. The inductive method leads potential reconcilers to ask questions, make informed observations, understand the historical context, form logical deductions and interpret the original and current meaning of a text. This information is then practically applied to the everyday life of an individual or group and in crosscultural interactions with others.

Fill up with God's Word as an act of ongoing engagement and partnership. Be open to experience the Word in new ways and to see and hear it with new eyes and ears. Appendix two of this book provides some Bible studies in Acts to help you do this. You will be further helped to see the Scriptures with new eyes if you are able to study them with people of different races, ethnicities or nationalities.

Our perspective on Scripture can also be enhanced when we pursue the discipline of studying other materials alongside the Bible. By reading books and watching videos we can explore stories of suffering brothers and sisters that will open our understanding. At the end of the book we offer a list of some of the books and videos that have challenged and changed us in our ongoing partnership.

As you read and watch these histories, listen to the cry of the poor and take note of the dignity of leaders who fought for reconciliation and justice, your heart and mind will be filled, and you will have much more insight and energy to give for the healing of people and the healing of nations.

RACIAL JUSTICE AND EVANGELISM

We desperately need a marriage between ministries of evangelism and ministries of racial reconciliation and justice. The proclamation and demonstration of the gospel *must* go together. People are tired of words that are not backed up by personal and social actions of compassion, service and justice. People today want to experience the gospel and see its impact for personal and social transformation before they want to hear our spiritual viewpoint. They want to see a message that *works* before they will consider responding in their own lives. *Experience* for people today must precede *explanation* if we are to gain a hearing for the gospel.[5]

As a result, many ministries today are pursuing compassion, service and justice as their primary way to awaken spiritual interest in the hearts of seekers and skeptics. InterVarsity, for instance, has a Spring Break project in partnership with Habitat for Humanity. The only requirement for being part of it is bringing along a pre-Christian friend. The impact on both believers and those who don't believe has been very powerful. Combining reconciliation, justice, and evangelism efforts puts the gospel back together and connects to the hearts of people in a culture who are tired of words without praxis.

We have seen how profound the call to conversion is when it happens in the context of a community seeking reconciliation and justice. Recently we ministered together at a weekend conference in the northwest United States. When the call to receive Christ was given, ten students stood up and came forward for prayer in front of the 350 students gathered. As we prayed for those ten students, we were amazed to see the depth and reality of their decisions to follow Christ. They were converting to the kingdom of God in all its multiethnic reality. They were not just praying an individualistic prayer. They were committing to personal and social transformation.

Communities that pursue justice and reconciliation proclaim the gospel with more credibility and power. And people that commit to follow Jesus in those communities often have a much more profound and radical conversion, both to God and to the kingdom of God's justice and love.

One other crucial dimension of this call to combine ministries of evangelism, justice and reconciliation relates to the great danger ministries of justice and compassion face. Those ministries often get caught up in activism and social change in ways that lead to burn out and to human-centered effort. We must always remember that it is God who builds his kingdom. We just get to work alongside God, filled with God's presence. And we must always remember that ultimately God's kingdom is not of this world. Sharing the good news about the salvation in Jesus that brings transformation in this life and relationship with God and one another forever keeps us healthy and spiritually vital as we pursue reconciliation and justice.

If you are involved in an urban project or an urban church, if you are serving the poor or partnering with people from other ethnic and racial backgrounds, we encourage you to keep a strong focus on evangelism and pursue that focus in practical ways. We have seen many ministries that lose their evangelistic edge begin to descend into burnout, lose their spiritual vitality and pursue a dependence on human activism rather than on the Spirit of God.

SPIRITUAL DISCIPLINES

Finally, it is important to recognize that in our work for justice and reconciliation, we often do not have control over the results. If our identity and our worth are wrapped up in our work and our success, we will rise and fall emotionally and spiritually and be ineffective in the battle for racial justice and ethnic reconciliation.

The practice of the sabbath reminds us that our worth is wrapped up in God. It brings us back home to the fact that our service is an act of worship—a responsive act of love to the One who gave his life for us. The sabbath is possibly the most fundamental Christian discipline, because it goes to the heart of our understanding of salvation. We are saved, given worth and identity, and promised a bright destiny by grace. We do not earn it. It is a gift. Sabbath uniquely leads us into *experiencing* the core of our conviction that we are saved by grace through faith and that is not of our own doing—so we rest.

Brenda observes this call to rest by taking a sabbath every Thursday for prayer, worship and reflection. She has felt called to do this for several years now. She is able to take a sabbath every Thursday because her ministry is also her job. If you work an eight-to-five job, or if sabbath observance is new to you, a sabbath/retreat day once a month may be more feasible for you. At times Brenda has kept her sabbath commitment well; at other times she has let life's demands, particularly the demands of funding the organization she founded, push her into anxiety to fill her life with activity. When she has kept her sabbath, it has been the centering place of her life. She can chart her capacity to face the demands of a ministry of racial reconciliation in reference to her faithfulness to the discipline of sabbath.

Celebration is another immensely needed discipline in our ongoing partnership. We need to celebrate our unity and our victories at least as often as we engage in repentance and mourning for all the efforts that have fallen short or gone wrong altogether. People who fight for justice seem especially handicapped in the discipline of celebration. At least annually, if not several times each year, throw a major party and have a massive celebration for all the good that God has done in bringing healing and justice through you and your ministry!

At one point Rick was working on a task force planning an evangelism conference, while at the same time, in the same room, another task force met to plan a conference on racial reconciliation and justice. The energy among the evangelists was bubbly, contagious and enthusiastic. It was also, no doubt, highly irritating to the justice group. They may have laughed or expressed positive energy once or twice, but those in the evangelism group never heard it if it happened. The members of the justice task force kept a very serious demeanor, often looked depressed and tended to get into arguments.

Facing injustice and working through relationships in which we have suffered immense wounds is not easy. It is hard work, and often the people involved won't feel good. However, as people are struggling through intense and difficult issues, they need the experience of grace, gratitude and celebration all the more. We certainly will mourn often, but in our work for justice and healing we need to practice the discipline of celebration, even if that doesn't come easily.

Consider celebrating by using spiritual disciplines and the sacraments in contexts that make them publicly prophetic and challenging. Hold celebration services in public places. Perhaps it would be especially meaningful to choose a place that symbolizes the rule of militarism, or materialism, or ethnocentrism, or empire building, or racial oppression. The cross is the defeat of all the powers, principalities and spirits that run rampant in our world. Through the practice of the sacraments we symbolically proclaim that the death and resurrection of Jesus Christ remain powerful and continue to challenge the principalities of our time. They also help us to enter into God's presence and his shalom to be restored and renewed.

Practice of the spiritual disciplines of celebration and worship lay at the heart of the civil rights movement, marked as it was by prayer and singing of hymns and spirituals that kept the protesters focused on God. What might have happened had those protesters not held worship services in church before going out to face vehement, degrading verbal and physical attacks? In the same way, in order to confront the prevailing spirits of our day we need to develop ongoing partnerships across denominational lines that help us to acknowledge and celebrate the person and work of Jesus Christ. What might happen if those of us who are committed to racial reconciliation began to hold Eucharist and prayer services in front of the New York or Chicago stock exchange to protest the unfair treatment of millions of people of color around the world? After taking Communion to symbolize our unity in Christ, we could encourage giving as a way to dethrone money and force the spirit of mammon into the service of God. All reality is one, and all acts are both spiritual and political as we collaborate with God to take back this world for his kingdom.

Consider organizing and hosting multiethnic healing celebrations. We believe such gatherings could usher in a new era of revival, refreshing and power for God's church. Help bring together citywide, multiethnic worship, prayer and proclamation gatherings. Brenda and Rick may want to join you! Explore healing, forgiveness, ethnic identity formation and spiritual warfare at small and large workshops and conferences. Invite God's Spirit to come, and receive God's healing. Use the gathering as an opportunity to proclaim God's victory over specific principalities and powers.

TAKING ACTION

God calls each of us to play a different role with different passions and gifts at various levels of intensity in the battle for ethnic healing and racial justice. However, if racial and ethnic reconciliation is to become an ongoing reality in our world, we must all intentionally take some action steps in that direction. Therefore we urge you to activate your commitment to racial and ethnic reconciliation by developing ongoing partnerships that will help you to continue your growth as a reconciler, guard you against burnout and support your lifestyle of racial righteousness. The following practical suggestions can help you on your journey to becoming a person God uses to facilitate the healing of people and the healing of nations.

1. Vote for political candidates who support economic justice and racial righteousness.

2. Volunteer to serve and use your skills and expertise (legal, accounting, cosmetology, carpentry or any other) in a nonprofit organization that promotes racial equality.

3. Give financial support to a ministry dedicated to racial justice and ethnic diversity.

4. Advocate for policies of hiring, promoting and supporting people from different racial and ethnic groups at your workplace.

5. Write a letter to the editor of your local newspaper to protest an incident of racial injustice or inequality in your community.

6. Organize an interracial sports league through your church to promote racial reconciliation among kids.

7. Sponsor a racial reconciliation rally with churches of different ethnicities in observance of Martin Luther King Day.

8. Build a home with others who stand for justice through Habitat for Humanity.

9. Invite international students from a nearby university to share their culture with you and your family during a holiday.

10. Join a multiracial church that is committed to social justice.

11. Tutor ESL (English as a Second Language) students.

12. Donate money to the local school library to purchase books that encourage racial and ethnic sensitivity and awareness.

13. Serve as a foster parent for children of different ethnicities.

14. Encourage your local school board to supply racial reconciliation curriculum, resources and training to classroom teachers and administrators in the district.

15. Volunteer in an urban ministry, and submit to and learn from leaders in the community.

16. Start a racial reconciliation reading and discussion group.

17. Sponsor a racial reconciliation film viewing and discussion group.

18. Serve in a short-term mission project under indigenous leadership in another country.

19. Learn about and support cottage-industry employment projects in other countries, such as the Heifer Project.

20. Learn about and celebrate holidays of people from other ethnicities.

21. Support a major initiative to benefit people of a different ethnic group in your community.

22. Host a diversity dinner or backyard barbecue for people from different racial groups in your neighborhood to get to know each other.

May God bless your efforts to take practical steps to pursue racial reconciliation and justice. Now let's pray.

God, we ask you to cleanse us of sentimental views of history and Scripture, of superficiality and racist attitudes and actions, and of our unwillingness to change. Grant a fresh wind of your Spirit to _____ [name your church, institution, country or community] and to our land, an energy to seek out the alien and stranger among us, to love in costly ways. Spare us from unfulfilled good intentions, and lead us to deeds that you yourself are doing, to your great glory and honor. Amen.[6]

THE TRUMPET CALL

Commissioning a Reconciliation Generation

This is a strategic time in history. It is time for us to embrace and exercise leadership as the Reconciliation Generation. Our calling was eloquently summarized by Dr. Martin Luther King Jr.:

> We will have to repent in this generation not merely for the hateful words and actions of the bad people but for the appalling silence of the good people. Human progress never rolls in on wheels of inevitability; it comes through the tireless efforts of men willing to be co-workers with God, and without this hard work, time itself becomes an ally of the forces of social stagnation. We must use time creatively, in the knowledge that the time is always ripe to do right. Now is the time to make real the promise of democracy and transform our pending national

elegy into a creative psalm of brotherhood. Now is the time to lift our national policy from the quicksand of racial injustice to the solid rock of human dignity.

The insights, tools and practical application strategies of the spiritual transformation model can equip and empower us to be more effective and successful in our fight for racial and ethnic reconciliation than any generation that has preceded us.

CALLING THE NEXT GENERATION OF LEADERS

Throughout this book we have called you to be coworkers with God as you redefine what power and authority are. Because of the abuses we have seen in prior generations, many postmoderns don't want authority, power or the limelight; instead we gravitate toward community and a "live and let live" approach. However, the world needs young leaders! We need you to transcend your individual reluctance to wield power in order to participate in a global movement. God wants to use you to be a part of the big picture, the great work he is doing throughout the earth. He is bringing forth his kingdom. So get over any personal indecision regarding whether you want to be involved, because *it's time!*

Sir Winston Churchill, prime minister of England during World War II, is credited with saying, "There comes a time in every person's life when they are given the unique opportunity to discover the purpose for which they were born. It is their moment of destiny. And if they seize it, it becomes their finest hour." God is doing something great in the earth, and he is looking for leaders who will seize the day. God's kingdom is coming on earth, and it will unite people from every tribe, language, ethnic group and nation. He invites us to get involved with what he is doing. This is our defining moment, and we must seize the day!

We challenge you to go beyond the safety and familiarity of your ethnic group in order to reach your full potential as agents of reconciliation and transformation in this needy, broken and hate-ridden world. This is a new season for leadership in the church. No longer will we be defined by a few charismatic superstar leaders at the center of all Christian activity. We are moving into a corporate model of leadership in this day. The new models of leadership that are emerging will be much more accountable to the communities they serve. In order to accomplish this, God is moving people forward into places of authority and responsibility. We must be ready to take a stand.

A CALLING TO FOLLOW GOD

Even if we let God give us the courage, saying yes will require hard work. It is not an easy task. That's why we are calling for a ministry of reconciliation that flows out of a *spirituality* of reconciliation. Its basis is the mystery of the incarnation: God, through the Son, makes room for humanity, once his enemy.

Many of our religious traditions have emerged from an "us versus them" mentality. We have defined our identity and pursued our security and dominance in the world by defining, excluding and ultimately annihilating the other. Repentance for sinner and sinned against consists in celebrating God's embrace of us, who were God's enemies, and then, out of the overflow of the experience of God's mercy, speaking the truth about our hurt and alienation and extending forgiveness and embrace to human others.

As we grow and develop our identity in dialogue, first with the ultimate Other, God, then also with the human others in our lives, we release our fears and embrace our new identity as God's agents of healing and transformation. This is our mission—to embrace a spirituality and ministry of reconciliation that is desperately needed in our conflict-ridden world.

We pray that our journey together into the spiritual transformation model of ethnic healing and racial justice has been a powerful experience for you. Remember that it is God who initiates and brings about reconciliation. We are colaborers with God. We cannot do this work in our own strength or ingenuity. Reconciliation is more a spirituality than a strategy. It is an ongoing spiritual process that involves forgiveness, repentance and justice to restore broken relationships to the way God intended them to be. Where the spiritual transformation model is applied, God's Spirit through the reconciliation process makes a new creation of both victim and oppressor. The result is authentic reconciliation and healing for the oppressor and the oppressed; they are liberated to be kingdom people who can be used by God to bring healing to people and nations.

It is our deepest prayer and belief that as we individually and corporately pursue the ministry of reconciliation—and as that ministry flows out of a deep spirituality that makes room for the other, including the enemy—our divided world will begin to see and experience God's kingdom. We believe that this is your mission, your assignment, and we boldly call you to it!

The trumpet call has sounded. It is your time to take your prophetic place in the plan of God, and we stand ready to commission you into your new identity as the Reconciliation Generation. God wants to use you to heal the soul of our nations.

As you heed the call and accept the challenge, we invite you to solidify your commitment by confessing and signing the Reconciliation Generation Covenant on the next page. Keep it as a reminder that you have joined the spiritual battle for racial and ethnic reconciliation.

As you prepare to apply the spiritual model of ethnic healing and racial justice, pray with us the prayer that Jesus gave:

Our Father in heaven,
hallowed be your name.
Your kingdom come, your will be done,
on earth as it is in heaven.
Give us this day our daily bread,
And forgive us our debts, as we also have forgiven our debtors.
And lead us not into temptation,
but deliver us from evil.
For yours is the kingdom, and the power, and the glory forever.
Amen.

RECONCILIATION
GENERATION COMMITMENT

In these opening years of the twenty-first century, we recognize that our world is becoming increasingly global and multiethnic. We are seeing a continued rise in suspicion, hostility and conflicts erupting between racial and ethnic groups around the world. We have experienced too many painful and destructive divisions in personal relationships, marriages, society, and among racial and ethnic groups.

But we know that our God is a God of reconciliation. When we became reconciled to God, we also became God's agents of reconciliation in the world. We want to stand together in this generation for the truth and power of the gospel of reconciliation. Our mission, should we choose to accept it, is to be coworkers with God to heal people and nations.

Therefore:

1. We commit ourselves to the **lordship** of Jesus Christ by pursuing a lifestyle of personal, ethnic and racial reconciliation.

2. We commit ourselves to reading **Scripture** with new eyes and responding with new hearts to God's call for reconciliation.

3. We commit ourselves to **prayer** by listening to God and praying to be filled with the Spirit to empower us for reconciliation.

4. We commit ourselves to **community** by building relationships that nurture our commitment to racial and ethnic reconciliation.

5. We commit ourselves to public **witness** by sharing our heart for reconciliation and by standing up for racial and ethnic justice.

This is my commitment before God.

Signature: _____ Date: _____

Brenda Salter McNeil and Rick Richardson, copyright 2000

APPENDIX 1

DEFINITIONS

CULTURE

"An integrated system of beliefs (about God, or reality, or ultimate meaning), of values (about what is true, good, beautiful, and normative), of customs (how to behave, relate to others, talk, pray, dress, work, play, trade, farm, eat, etc.), and of institutions which express these beliefs, values and customs (governments, law courts, temples or churches, family, schools, hospitals, factories, shops, unions, clubs, etc.), which binds a society together and gives it a sense of identity, dignity, security, and continuity."[1]

ETHNICITY

"Ethnic groups are human groups which cherish a belief in their common origins of such a kind that it provides a basis for the creation of community."[2]

"Of or relating to large groups of people classed according to common racial, national, tribal, religious, linguistic, or cultural origin or background" (Merriam-Webster Dictionary).

Ethnicity is derived from the Greek word ethnos, which literally means tribe, nation or people group. It connotes sharing the same habits or customs. Ethnicity is therefore a common cultural heritage that is maintained by a group of people that distinguishes them from others. Every person has an ethnicity, which is identified by language, social views, common history, rituals, characteristics, customs and beliefs. One's ethnicity is held in common with other members of one's group and may be reflected religiously, racially, geographically, culturally or nationally.

Primarily this book is about healing your ethnic identity and about reconciling diverse and embattled ethnic groups.

RACE

This term refers to the belief that natural and separate divisions, akin to subspecies, exist within humankind.

The commonly held definition of *race* is "any of the different varieties or populations of human beings distinguished by physical traits such as hair, eyes, skin color, body shape, etc."[3] However, it is generally accepted by sociologists, anthropologists and biologists that race is a social construct and not a biological reality. There seem to be no meaningful biological criteria that distinguish one group of people from another.

The concept of race was a social construct used to systematically stigmatize certain people groups as inferior, thus justifying racial slavery, injustice and inequality. We will use race as a category because it is a socially understood term.

Racial characteristics are just one set of characteristics that have necessarily developed out of the spread of human groups to different regions and continents with varying geographies, weather conditions and economic opportunities.

Here's one report on race that illustrates the origin and dynamics of racial differences.

We are 99.99% the same genetically. The remaining .01% is not differentiation along racial lines for the most part. 85% of it is differentiation within and not between groups. Africans are the most genetically varied, and are probably [from] the initial birthplace of humanity. We all share the same African mother. The European gene pool is a swirl of 35% African and 65% Asian genes.[4]

A quick review of how racial classification developed is helpful here:

Race as a category emerged in the Enlightenment out of the effort to categorize and differentiate all species of life. French physician Francois Bernier (1620-1688) identified Europeans (Caucasians), Far Easterners, "blacks" and Lapps (Native American). Carolus Linnaeus (1707-1778), a Swedish professor of botany, appropriated the Aristotelian categories of genus and species to divide the human species into Europeans, Asians, Africans and Americans (Native). Linnaeus was the first to emphasize color: white, yellow, black and red people to go with the classifications. Johann Friedrich Blumenbach (1752-1840) is credited with the term *Caucasian* for the European race, from the discovery of a particularly aesthetically pleasing skull he found in the Caucasus Mountains. They classified the races with a bias toward the superiority of European culture, and toward establishing a basis for that superiority in biology. The classification ended up being interpreted as a hierarchy of superordination and subordination, legitimating discrimination, violation, isolation and extermination.[5]

There has been a big debate around race and racism. "Can people of color be racist?" is the question that is often asked. The question, and the tone in which it is often asked, betrays an ignorance of history. Racial consciousness as such didn't even exist until Europeans created it in order to justify a doctrine of their superiority and dominance in the world. Ethnocentrism, the belief that my ethnic group is central, superior and destined to dominate, has characterized many ethnic groups throughout history. Anyone can be ethnocentric. Ethnocentrism was one of the main barriers to the spread of the gospel beyond the Jewish people, as recorded in the book of Acts. But *racism,* the belief that my *race* is inherently superior, is a peculiarly European and European American creation, and therefore Europeans are uniquely responsible for the evil of racism. Racism is central to the expression of the Fall and of self-worship in the nations whose roots go back to Europe. Racism is Europe's and America's racialized ethnocentrism. Europeans and their descendants used racial differences as determinative categories to unite Europeans and their descendants in efforts to dominate the rest of the world.

RACIALIZATION

"Refers to the culture and practices of a society that institutionalize, perpetuate and reinforce a situation 'wherein race matters profoundly for differences in life experiences, life opportunities and social relationships.' A racialized society 'allocates differential economic, political, social, and even psychological rewards to groups along racial lines: lines that are socially constructed.'"[6]

Race as a category was born out of the European scientific and cultural drive toward power and conquest, roughly from 1492 (Columbus's discovery and beginning conquest of the Americas) to 1945 at the end of World War II, when the colonies of the world began to break free.

Race and racism were key means for establishing, maintaining and justifying relationships of dominance by Europeans of all non-European ethnic groups and nations on the basis of the "inferiority" of those other ethnic groups and nations. Race and racism are expressions of the fall of a people, in particular the fall of the European peoples, and their descent into idolatry: the worship of power and the pursuit of dominance in the world.

ETHNOCENTRISM

This is an emotional attitude and belief system that maintains that one's own ethnic group, culture or race is superior to others.

RACISM

We have adapted the following definition from Karen McKinney of Bethel College in Minnesota: "Racism is the belief in the superiority of one race and the inferiority of other races, leading to the collective misuse of power that results in diminished life opportunities for some racial groups."[7]

STEREOTYPING

A fixed and distorted generalization about all members of a particular group, ignoring any individual differences.

PEOPLE OF COLOR

Inclusive term for African Americans, Caribbean Americans, Asian Americans, Japanese, Koreans, Pakistanis, Pacific Islanders, American Indians, Latinas/Latinos, Chicanas/Chicanos and the like. The term may not be preferred by everyone. Ask for preferences when possible.

WHITE PRIVILEGE

Simply put, white privilege is the package of benefits granted to people in our society who have white skin—a parcel of privileges white people have been granted, which allow them certain things in our society that are not easily available to people of color.

RECONCILIATION

An ongoing spiritual process involving forgiveness, repentance and justice that restores broken relationships to the way God intended them to be.

RECONCILIATION GENERATION BIBLE STUDIES

For Small Group or One-on-One Study

1. LORDSHIP

Passage to Explore: Acts 1:6-8

We commit ourselves to the **lordship** of Jesus Christ by pursuing a lifestyle of personal, ethnic and racial reconciliation.

a. Reflect on and discuss your experiences with people of other cultures and ethnicities. Have you had good experiences, negative experiences or not much experience?

b. Read Acts 1:6-8. What do the disciples ask Jesus?

c. How do they betray their ethnocentric focus?

d. How does Jesus answer their questions about dates and their focus on their own ethnic group?

e. What would the disciples have felt about each of the groups Jesus says they will be witnesses to? How do you think they may have felt about this commission?

Note: Jerusalem was the center of the world for the disciples. Each concentric circle out took the disciples to people who were more despised. So this commission would not be good news for these ethnocentric believers.

f. What does this passage say to you about who you are called to reach on your campus or in your community?

g. How are the people in your campus fellowship, church or small group like the disciples? In what ways has your group chosen to only care about people from your background?

h. How might God be calling you to change in response to the lordship of Christ?

2. SCRIPTURE

Passage to Explore: Acts 6:1-7

We commit ourselves to reading *Scripture* with new eyes and responding with new hearts to God's call for reconciliation.

a. Do you think ethnic and racial reconciliation are important themes in the Scriptures? What passages do you know that address these issues?

b. Read Acts 6:1-7. What is the problem that arises in the early church? How is this a cultural or ethnic issue? How is it a justice issue?

c. How do the disciples solve the problem they are facing? What are the characteristics of the men they choose to solve the problem?

d. What is the cultural background of the men they choose to solve the problem? Do you think that's important? Why or why not?
Note: The names of these men are *Greek* names, not Hebrew names. So Hellenistic Jews, who were considered less pure than Hebrew Jews, were given the task of serving all the widows, Hellenistic and Hebrew.

e. Who now serves the Hebraic widows, who were originally being taken care of so well, and why might that be significant?

f. How does the resolution of this crisis affect the spread of the gospel?

g. Who do you want to reach out to on your campus or in your community? How might this model of sharing power and involving people in meeting their own needs help you in reaching them?

h. Have you ever studied the Bible with these kinds of questions in mind? In your personal Bible study this week, look at how God uses Stephen and Philip in crosscultural ministry over the next several chapters of Acts.

3. PRAYER

Passage to Explore: Acts 10:1-48

We commit ourselves to *prayer* by listening to God and praying to be filled with the Spirit to empower us for reconciliation.

a. What experiences have you had of hearing God speak to you? What impact has that had on your life?

b. Read Acts 10:1-48. Why does God choose Cornelius? What is Cornelius doing when he hears from God?

c. What was Peter doing and thinking about when he had the vision?

d. What do you notice about Peter's vision and the voice? Why do you think it happens three times?

e. What do you notice about the coming of the three men and the conversation? Why might it have been significant that Peter invited them in?

f. Talk about the different things God does in here in a supernatural way. Why do you think God does each of those things?

g. How does Cornelius respond to the things God does supernaturally?

h. How does Peter respond to the things God does supernaturally? How does Peter change?

i. How does listening to God affect Cornelius and Peter and their response to each other and each other's cultural background? How were they at first resistant to what God wanted to do to bring them together, and how did they change?

j. Spend some time sharing your experiences in cross-ethnic and crosscultural relationships, how God has worked in them and how you would like to see God work. Then pray for each other. Particularly pray about any crosscultural encounters that were hard. Make sure also to spend time in quiet prayer, listening to God, and share with each other anything you think God might be saying to you.

4. COMMUNITY

Passages to Explore: Acts 11:19-30; 13:1-3; 14:26-28

We commit ourselves to *community* by building relationships that nurture our commitment to racial and ethnic reconciliation

a. How multiethnic is your church, fellowship or small group? What would it take for your church or group to become a truly multiethnic fellowship? Is God calling you in that direction?

b. Read Acts 11:19-30. How did the church at Antioch get started? Who started the church, and why might that be significant?

c. What do you know about Barnabas and the kind of man he was? What equipped him to go evaluate and then help lead the first truly multiracial church? You can refer to the end of Acts 4 and to Acts 9:27-30.

d. Why do you think it might be significant that the disciples were first called Christians at Antioch? What characterizes these people?

e. Read Acts 13:1-3 and 14:26-28. How does the leadership here reflect the church, and why might that be important?

f. Why do you think God uses this church to launch Barnabas and Paul in mission to the Gentiles?

g. Read through Acts 13—15, either now or during the next week. What impact does this multiracial church have on the spread of the gospel?

h. How would you like to grow or see your group grow in becoming more like the Antioch church? How might that affect the relationships in your life?

i. What step do you want to take in developing a cross-ethnic or cross-racial relationship? Pray for each other.

5. WITNESS

Passage to Explore: Galatians 2:11-21

We commit ourselves to public *witness* by sharing our heart for reconciliation and by standing up for racial and ethnic justice.

a. Whom do you know who has taken a costly stand for something he or she believed in? What impact did that person have on you?

b. Skim through Galatians 1:1—2:10 then read 2:11-21. What is the context for Galatians 2:11-21? What conflict does Paul face? Why would this situation have been hard for Paul?

c. What does Peter do? Why do you think he does that? What is the impact on others?

d. What threat to the gospel and to Paul's life work do Peter's actions represent?

e. What was Paul's answer to Peter and to the Jewish people who thought a person needed to be circumcised to be saved (see Acts 15:1)?

f. What objection to Peter's understanding of the gospel does Paul respond to in 2:17? What is Paul's response?

g. What will happen to the gospel and to the centrality of Jesus' death on the cross if Paul lets Peter get away with separating himself culturally from the Greeks?

h. Respond to the following statement:

> Our God is a God of reconciliation. Ethnocentrism and racism always carry with them an understanding of salvation that violates the truth of the gospel and the necessity of the cross. Whenever our community reinforces splitting the new humanity back into its separate and alienated parts, the gospel has been undone!

How do you see this statement relating to this passage in Galatians?

i. What steps do you want to take to make racial and ethnic reconciliation a more ongoing part of your life and your Christian community?

j. How do you personally want to express your commitment to ethnic and racial reconciliation?

APPENDIX 3

THE PRINCIPALITIES
AND POWERS

For those readers who want a more theologically profound engagement with the issue of just what principalities and powers are in the Scriptures, and how these biblical ideas can be seen in our culture, here is a further bit of background.

Four key thinkers inform our perspective on the principalities and powers, and we recommend them as further reading:

1. Marva Dawn, *Powers, Weakness, and the Tabernacling of God* (Grand Rapids, Mich.: Eerdmans, 2001);

2. Robert Linthicum, *City of God, City of Satan* (Grand Rapids, Mich.: Zondervan, 1991);

3. William Stringfellow, *An Ethic for Christians and Other Aliens in a Strange Land* (Waco, Tex.: Word, 1973); and *Free in Obedience* (New York: Seabury, 1964); and

4. Walter Wink in his Powers trilogy: *Engaging the Powers* (Minneapolis: Fortress, 1992); *Naming the Powers* (Philadelphia: Fortress, 1984); and *Unmasking the Powers* (Philadelphia: Fortress, 1986).

KEY BIBLICAL TEXTS

Here is a concise overview of how Scripture characterizes the principalities and powers. We have synthesized this overview from Marva Dawn's work cited above.

- Colossians 1:6: The powers are created for good.

- Romans 8:19-22: As part of the fallen creation, the powers share in its brokenness, participate in its destructions, overstep their proper bounds, and groan for release.

- Romans 8:38-39: No matter how strong, the powers cannot separate us from God's love in Christ.

- 1 Corinthians 15:25-26: Death is one of the cosmic enemies to be subjected to Christ.

- Colossians 2:13-15: Christ disarmed the powers, exposed them, and triumphed over them.

- 1 Peter 3:22: Powers and authorities (grouped here with angels, which prevents us from losing sight of their larger dimensions beyond earthly materiality) are made subject to Christ.

- 1 Corinthians 2:8 : The other side of the dialectic is given here: that earthly rulers (principalities) crucified the Lord of glory. This text also underscores the powers' functioning in religious, as well as political, spheres. This alerts us to the disturbing fact that churches today can similarly be principalities acting for evil instead of good.

- Ephesians 6:10-20: We must stand against the powers and resist them by means of the armor of God.

WHAT ARE THE POWERS?

Essentially, principalities and powers are the authorities and rulers of the world. They include angelic and demonic personalities, human personalities like kings and presidents and corporate groupings like nations. For instance, Babylon in Scripture is a principality, even though it is neither a demonic personality nor a human king. These principalities were created by God, according to Colossians 1:16, and therefore were good in their initial state.

In what sense did Christ create the principalities and powers? Clearly, Christ did not create governments and nations and kings initially, but only Adam and Eve as the first family. Christ is the creator of the powers themselves, those demonic and angelic forces behind the systems. But Christ also created the underlying need and even template in humanity to structure, systematize and order its life together, as the expression of the image of God to fill and subdue creation.[1] So humans created kinship groupings and nations, but did so out of the template of human nature, created by God, in the image of God. So the creation of humanity and the command to be fruitful and multiply ultimately includes the development of the earthly structures and institutions that rule our lives. These structures of our existence had a good purpose in the mind and intention of God. Of course, these structures of existence are now bent toward human self-rule and self-glorification. They need to be redeemed, brought back under the gracious rule of God. When God's kingdom comes in fullness, human and angelic rulers, corporate structures, and ruling ideas will all collaborate together for the glory of God and the service of all creation.

Paul summarizes the breadth of the reality of the principalities and powers in Ephesians 6:12 when he says: "For our struggle is not against flesh and blood, but against the rulers, against the authorities, against the powers of this dark world and against the spiritual forces of evil in the heavenly realms." Paul here describes these rulers as heavenly and earthly. They are the people and forces and angelic/demonic rulers and authorities who influence us. Our tendency in the West is to view these forces as only material and to ignore the demonic personalities that stand behind earthly rulers. But the biblical worldview holds all these dimensions of reality together. The material, institutional, social and spiritual dimensions all work together. This whole-cloth vision of reality is much more profound and powerful than the merely materialistic view so common in Western culture.

Biblically, the powers (human, institutional and demonic rulers) propagate social myths that have immense power and influence in our lives. The myth of Mammon, for instance, the myth that we can achieve true security from all danger and true control of our world through the accumulation of wealth, is false and deceptive and ultimately very destructive. We need to understand that this myth, upheld by the human, demonic and institutional rulers of our society, must be exposed and rejected and renounced (that is, demythologized). This act of prophetic courage and clear-sightedness is the true intention of the biblical language of principalities and powers.

The Triumph of the Cross

Satan is a defeated foe, as are all the principalities and powers. They have been defeated at the cross. Addressing the demonic and idolatrous powers of the Law and of religion, the writer of Colossians tells us that God "forgave us all our sins, having canceled the written code, with its regulations, that was against us and that stood opposed to us; he took it away, nailing it to the cross. And, having disarmed the powers and authorities, he made a public spectacle of them, tri-

175

umphing over them by the cross" (2:13-15). Yet the powers are still very influential in our world. Their power has been broken, their sovereignty limited, but they are "fighting like Hell to restore their autonomy from God."[2] Their legitimacy to rule has been cancelled at the cross, and their true nature as enemies of God has been exposed. But they carry on, through human people, human ideologies and human institutions that are willing to live the lies that they propagate.

In the end, these rogue principalities and powers must be brought back together into submission to God. And so, according to Ephesians 1:10 and 1:22, all things must again be brought together under one Head, even Christ. All things must be put back under his feet. This dethronement of rebellious principalities and powers happened in a real sense at the rising and ascension of Jesus (Ephesians 1:21), but this submission of all things to Christ must be consummated in the age to come, when the times have reached their fulfillment (Ephesians 1:10). At that time, *all* things will be reconciled, things in heaven and earth, things visible and invisible. All things, including all the principalities and powers that are redeemable, will be reconciled and brought back together under one head, even Christ.

It should be noted that some powers, like death and sin, will not be redeemed but rather destroyed. These powers in the world are rebellious to the core, against Life in every way. These powers were not initially part of God's good creation or God's good intention. And even Satan, who was initially part of God's creation, will be destroyed. In an age that wants to reconcile everything, and wants to reject the reality of evil, it is very important to say that some powers are irredeemable and irreconcilable.

But most of the powers in our world will find the fulfillment of their intended role in God's future. And their redemption has begun now, as they see the power of the gospel proclaimed and lived out before their watching eyes. That's why the writer of Ephesians said, "His intent was that now, through the church, the manifold wisdom of God should be made known to the rulers and authorities in the heavenly realms" (3:10).

In context, this verse tells us that Jewish/Gentile unity in the church is a message to the rebellious principalities and powers. The message to these powers is this: the equal access that both Jews and Gentiles have to God through Christ demonstrates and proves to watching principalities and powers how many-splendored is God's wisdom. Formerly hostile groups of people who become reconciled through the power of the cross are the best evangelistic message we can preach! The medium is the message! And that message is preached not only to people, but also to the watching rebellious principalities and powers.

How are we to fight the battle against these principalities and powers? We are to proclaim the cross and live the cross. We proclaim the victory of Christ. And we show that victory, not through our own power, but through God's power demonstrated in our weakness. As Marva Dawn puts it so well:

> We are to be like the little child who cries, "But he has no clothes on at all." But instead, we in the church have often turned victory into a new autonomous power. The worship service can be seen as spiritual battle: the sermon names the powers and demonstrates their perversions, the offering attacks the power of money, intercession commits us to live out our freedom, sacraments give signs and seals of our triumph in Christ.[3]

Even as Christ accomplished victory through weakness, suffering and death, so the Lord accomplishes witness to the world through weakness. God has more need of our weakness than of our strength. Just as the powers overstep their bounds and become gods, so our power becomes a rival to God. By our union with Christ in the power of the Spirit in our weaknesses, we display God's glory.[4]

And Marva Dawn asks us a very haunting question about our formulation of the gospel in the West in her book on the principalities and powers: *"How have the very powers themselves conspired to leave us with a gospel and ethic that perpetuates their control?"* Dawn's question is very important for us. Put simply: Are the forces of spiritual and demonic power happy that we preach an individualistic gospel that leaves out their role and the necessity of renouncing their influence? This question is absolutely vital for us. May we have the courage to face this question, search our hearts and respond!

EXPLORING THE HEART
OF RACIAL JUSTICE

A Strategic Tool for Leaders

Brenda Salter McNeil with Sharisse K. Jones

INTRODUCTION

In order for any organization, institution or group to change, change must first occur in its leader. When the head gets in line, the body must follow. This guide provides leaders with a blueprint for a change strategy to aid them in their journey. Groups or teams can read the book together, and the leader can use the guide to make the process a strategic one.

The questions are divided according to the following types of leadership: self leadership, group leadership and organizational leadership.

Self leadership is the leadership authority we all possess over our own selves. It is the capacity to shape and guide our own lives, thoughts and attitudes. A leader must first take the blinders off his or her own eyes so that she can effectively guide others. The questions in this section will provide a framework through which the leader can understand the process of racial reconciliation as a personal journey, as a precursor to leading a group or organization through the same process. It is our intention that the leader will utilize these questions in a time of quiet and personal reflection, in preparation to facilitate the discussions generated by the group leadership and organizational leadership questions. It would be helpful to use a journal to record the answers to these questions.

Group leadership includes leadership of a small group, classroom or ministry. There are unique opportunities that exist in these more intimate settings, which when properly realized, can become powerful vehicles for racial reconciliation. The questions in this section will help the group leader identify opportunities for facilitating racial reconciliation and will offer tools to help the group achieve true community. These are discussion questions that the leader can use to spark and stimulate discussion with the group or team.

Larger questions, which address macrolevel issues, are offered for consideration in the organizational leadership section. In this way, the leader of an institution, denomination or organization can begin to identify potential areas for improvement in his organization as it relates to racial justice. These questions are application oriented, and they are written to provide opportunities for brainstorming toward practical steps that an organization or institution can take in the journey toward racial reconciliation.

Activities are suggested to provide concrete application opportunities, as well as insight into the complexities of the challenges inherent in achieving racial reconciliation. The activities and concluding prayer also provide a focal point for leaders as they continue to guide groups, ministries and organizations toward racial justice.

The work to be done in each chapter can be accomplished in one hour. Of course, if you have more time, you have the opportunity to delve even deeper into the topics and questions suggested. However, I am confident that a meaningful process can result from using the following time allocation for each chapter:

Activity:	15 minutes
Self-leadership questions:	Pregroup time by leader alone
Group Questions:	20 minutes
Organization Questions:	20 minutes
Prayer:	5 minutes

Each section concludes by referring the leader to the prayers that close each chapter of the book. As racial reconciliation is a spiritual problem, which requires spiritual solutions, it is imperative to maintain a God-centered focus throughout this journey. We also recommend that each group or team participant record his or her thoughts/impressions/answers/questions in a journal throughout this process, as a tool for later reflection and thought. Additionally, I encourage you to select a participant to serve as a scribe, who will take notes at each session, to be kept by the leader in a notebook or binder. This book will serve as a tangible outcome of the group's work and can be used for later reflection and as a potential resource for enacting the ideas and suggestions that result from the organizational-leadership brainstorming sessions.

Let us begin.

CHAPTER 1. IS THERE STILL A RACE PROBLEM?

Activity

Invite each person to reflect on a time when something important was learned about racial and ethnic difference. Ask each participant to think about what happened, what was learned, and the response. Ask each participant to write down his or her experience on an $8\frac{1}{2}$ x 11 sheet of paper and bring it to the group. Once everyone is assembled, invite each participant to share his or her experience. Collectively discuss your reactions to these experiences and how they affect your agreement to the authors' proposal that a race problem still exists. After the discussion, collect all of the papers and place them in a notebook or binder.

Discussion

Self Leadership (reflect on these questions alone and record your answers in a journal)

- How does the knowledge that there is still a race problem influence the way that you lead those of various racial and ethnic backgrounds?

- Does this knowledge affect your perception of certain situations or experiences of your group or ministry?

Group Leadership (use these questions to facilitate a group discussion)

- Do you believe that a race problem still exists? Why or why not?

- What in your personal experience has informed your answer to this question?

- Page 20 of *The Heart of Racial Justice* describes the disparity in the way people of color and white people perceive the existence of a race problem. Why do you think this disparity still exists?

Organizational Leadership (use these questions to incite a brainstorming session)

- In what ways has your organization, church or institution ignored or combated the existence of a race problem?

- Given the insidious nature of the race problem that still exists in America, how can your organization, church or institution begin to empower its members so that your organization, church or institution becomes a haven from such outside hostilities? Once this is accomplished, how then can your organization, church or institution become an agent of change in your community?

- How diverse is your organization, church or institution? Does the diversity reflect the diversity of America? Why or why not? What can you do to make your organization, church or institution more reflective of America's racial and ethnic diversity?

Prayer

Please refer to the prayer on page 23.

CHAPTER 2. MISSION IMPOSSIBLE?

Activity

As you normally watch television during the course of one week, take particular note of the diversity of the cast of the television shows you watch. Discuss whether the diversity in the world of television reflects the diversity of American society. Do you think it should? What are the effects, if any, of the diversity (or lack thereof) you currently see in the media?

Discussion

Self Leadership

- When considering the magnitude of the race problem in America, do you ever feel overwhelmed or complacent? What can you do to help combat those feelings? How can you tap into the power of God to help you?

- What strategies can you implement as a leader to stave off feelings of being overwhelmed and helpless in the struggle toward racial reconciliation?

Group Leadership

- What does racial reconciliation mean to you?

- How can a soul change in you lead to social change in your environment?

- Identify a way in which your group or team can measure your success in your journey toward racial justice.

- How does the knowledge that racism is a spiritual problem inform how you attack it within your group or ministry?

Organizational Leadership

- Does your organization, church or institution contain members of the "emerging generation"? How can you utilize members of this group to respond to this *kairos* moment in history?

- Do you see any vestiges that the generational sin of racism has infiltrated your organization, church or institution? Where? How?

Prayer
Please refer to the prayer on page 31.

CHAPTER 3. A BETTER WAY

Activity
Read Revelation 21—22. Invite members of your team, group or or-

ganization to reflect on the unique giftedness and goodness of their respective cultures and ethnic groups, and ask them to bring in a physical representation (e.g., a photograph) that can be used by the group to create a collage or mosaic, representing the beauty and uniqueness of all of the cultures and ethnic groups in your ministry or organization. When completed, this collage or mosaic can be displayed in an area suited for reflection and remembrance of the inherent value of each ethnic and cultural group to God and, likewise, the treasure each brings to your organization, ministry or institution.

Discussion

Self Leadership

- How can you embrace the ethnic and racial identity of those whom you lead in a way that values each group without creating disunity?

- Are you able to value your racial and ethnic identity while still submitting it to the identity of being in Christ's family? Have you ever felt that you have had to abandon your racial and ethnic identity in order to be a "good" Christian?

- Have you ever operated from an ethnocentric perspective? In what ways have you seen this evidenced in your life? How is this opposed to the message of the gospel?

Group Leadership

- Do you believe that there can be unity without sameness? In what ways does your team, ministry or group reflect this?

- What is your self-image? To what degree does it come from a vertical perspective that you are valuable to God?

Organizational Leadership

• How has the church been silent in the face of racism and racial injustice? How can you work as a leader to insure that your organization, institution or church is an active force for racial reconciliation?

• How can Christian institutions or organizations move toward embracing and valuing diversity?

• What steps can we take to escape cultural homogeneity as we reach out to others from different racial and ethnic backgrounds?

• Does your church or organization reflect unity in diversity, or does it reflect unity in homogeneity? What would most help your group move toward the unity in diversity that Scripture commands (e.g., Ephesians 2:11-16; 4:11-18)?

Prayer

Please refer to the prayer on page 43.

CHAPTER 4. A NEW MODEL

Activity

Invite members of your team or group to write a clear and concise definition of the healing model of racial reconciliation. How does it differ from the interpersonal model or institutional change model? Discuss the strengths and weaknesses of each model and give historical examples of each. (For example, under which model would the civil rights movement fall?)

Discussion

Self Leadership

• Do you have any interpersonal relationships across ethnic and racial lines? If so, how have these relationships challenged your views about race and ethnicity? How have you been able to use these relationships to advance your knowledge of and sensitivity toward race issues?

- Do you believe that applying the interpersonal model is the most effective method of transforming race relations? Why or why not?

Group Leadership

- How does the healing model of racial reconciliation differ from the interpersonal model and the institutional change model? How can the healing model complement the interpersonal and institutional models? With which model is your group or ministry identified?

- How does racial reconciliation differ from racial tolerance and political correctness? Are the latter valid steps along the journey toward racial reconciliation or merely superficial substitutes for true change?

- Why is God's presence essential to the healing model of racial reconciliation?

Organizational Leadership

- Has your organization or institution adopted the institutional change model to effect racial reconciliation? How successful has it been? What are the strengths and weaknesses of this model?

- Can the healing model compliment the institutional change model? How?

- Are there ways in which your organization or institution can create opportunities for telling the truth?

Prayer

Please refer to the prayer on page 58.

CHAPTER 5. HOW WORSHIP BUILDS BRIDGES

Activity

"Plan" a multiracial, multicultural worship or prayer service. What elements would you include to allow all of the attendees to bring their whole selves to the worship experience? What kind of music would you select? What kind of prayers? Which Scripture readings? What kinds of things would you include in the liturgy? How would you create an atmosphere of "unity in diversity"?

Discussion

Self Leadership

- How can worship be transformative? What is intensified and magnified when we worship? What is consumed?

- How important is honesty in worship? What is revealed in us individually as we worship?

- In what ways can you practice the presence of God?

- How is worship an essential step in the journey toward racial reconciliation?

- Is worship a spiritual activity or a lifestyle? Explain.

Group Leadership

- How are ethnocentrism and racism antithetical to worship? How does worship help destroy these attitudes?

- How does worship help us embrace the possibility of racial reconciliation?

- How important is it for people of various racial and ethnic groups to come together in worship? What does unity in multiethnic worship look like? sound like?

- What attitudes do we need to cultivate for our worship to become an experience that unites us rather than an issue that divides us?

Organizational Leadership

- How can your institution or organization become a place where God's presence is practiced in such a way that the atmosphere is ripe for reconciliation?

- How does worship equip us to live counterculturally? How can your organization utilize worship as a tool to create prophets who criticize the world's status quo?

- How can your organization authentically reflect a kingdom made up of people from every tribe, every language and every nation?

Prayer
Please refer to the prayer on pages 70-72.

CHAPTER 6. EMBRACING OUR TRUE SELVES

Activity
Bring a hand mirror. While sitting in a circle, ask each member of your team or group to look at themselves in the mirror and complete the following statement: When I look into the mirror, I see _____ and it makes me feel _____.

Decipher and discuss to which false identity (found on pages 77-89) each statement points.

Discussion

Self Leadership

- Do you believe that your cultural heritage and racial background are important aspects of your Christian identity? Why or why not?

- What false identities have been used to define you? Do you see how false identities, which cause you to bend toward other people or groups or even to your own group, are a form of idolatry?

Group Leadership

- What is your true identity? How can you reclaim it? To whom must you look? What do you need in order to live out of your true identity?

- How can your group or ministry use words to speak truth and encourage others toward becoming new creations by celebrating their racial identity in Christ?

- How important is it for the individuals in your group to embrace their cultural identity in Christ so that your group can effectively lead others to a celebration of their racial and cultural identity in Christ?

Organizational Leadership

- Has your organization or institution unknowingly "discipled" people out of their racial and ethnic identities, as if they were unimportant to their Christian faith? If yes, how so? In what ways have you observed this?

- Do you believe that a subtle form of white-supremacist false identity infects all European Americans? Do you see any consequences of this false identity in your organization?

Prayer

Please refer to the prayers on pages 92-93.

CHAPTER 7. RECEIVING AND EXTENDING FORGIVENESS

Activity

Invite each member to read an experience shared in chapter one (it does not necessarily have to be their own). After each experience is read, tear the corresponding pages from the notebook or binder and place them in a glass bowl or other fireproof container. After all of the experiences have been read, invite the group to gather in a circle around the container with the written pages. Invite one person to offer a prayer seeking forgiveness on behalf of those who perpetrated the harms, and ask another person to offer a prayer receiving forgiveness on behalf of everyone who experienced the discrimination. Burn, or otherwise destroy, the pages as the leader prays a blessing over the memories, seeking God for healing and strength.

Discussion

Self Leadership

- Have you experienced or benefited from "white privilege"?
- Do you believe that those who benefit from a crime share in the responsibility of that crime and need to help make things right? Why or why not?

- How can your group address the need for collective healing of memories? Are there ways to facilitate this type of healing?

- How necessary is forgiveness to the healing model of racial reconciliation and to the eradication of crosscultural trust issues?

- In what ways can your group work to erase crosscultural trust issues?

Organizational Leadership

- What is necessary in order for there to be an environment of trust and vulnerability so that hurt, rage and hopelessness can be laid at the foot of the cross? Do you feel that such an environment exists within your organization or institution?

Prayer

Revisit the section titled "Making a Full Confession: Receiving Cleansing and Healing," found on pages 109-10.

CHAPTER 8. DENOUNCING THE POWERS AND PRINCIPALITIES

Activity

Invite members of your team, group or ministry to get a copy of today's edition of your local newspaper. Ask each individual to identify the powers and principalities (spirit of pride, spirit of the empire, spirit of fear and spirit of mammon) that appear to be manifesting in the different stories reflecting current events. Discuss.

Discussion

Self Leadership

- What is your response to the assertion that racism is a principality or a demonic power? Do you believe it? Why or why not?

- In what ways is racism rooted in the spirit of pride? Do you see a connectedness between ethnocentricity and pride and idolatry?

- Are there certain institutions that you can identify that reinforce a sense of chosenness, specialness and a right to dominate others?

- What images have you observed that reinforce that sense of chosenness, specialness and the right to dominate others?

Group Leadership

- In what ways is the spirit of fear manifested in racism? What can you do within your group or ministry to expose this spirit and combat it?

- How can your ministry or group more effectively disciple nations and not just individuals?

- How can your ministry or group reach the marginalized in your city or larger community?

- Why is a sense of humor important in waging the spiritual battle against the principalities and powers behind racism?

Organizational Leadership

- Are there institutional forces you can identify within your organization or institution, which reinforce a sense of chosenness, specialness and a right to dominate others? What are the ideologies that support those institutions?

- Which groups are being marginalized as a result of the ideologies and institutions that reinforce a sense of chosenness and specialness?

- What are some ways to better reach those who have been marginalized and left out of God's kingdom?

Prayer

Revisit and renounce the powers using the prayer found on pages 131-32.

CHAPTER 9. ONGOING PARTNERSHIPS

Activity

Identify another individual, church, ministry or organization that shares your commitment to racial reconciliation. Identify one of the activities listed on pages 150-52 that you would like to engage in with this identified organization, ministry, church or individual. As you plan, discuss potential obstacles to the practical application of your commitment to racial reconciliation. What appears to be easy; what seems more difficult? What barriers do you foresee?

Discussion

Self Leadership

- Have you ever submitted to the leadership of a person who was from a different ethnic and racial background? What was that experience like for you? Was it difficult or challenging?
- Have you ever left your community in order to help others?
- How would you rate your intercultural communication skills? What can you do to improve them?

Group Leadership

- In order to develop ongoing partnerships, it is imperative to identify with others of various ethnic and racial groups as unique individuals, not just members of a group. In what ways can your group or ministry create such opportunities?

- What kind of information-gathering and critical-thinking activities can your group or ministry engage in to educate your members about the causes of crosscultural conflict?

- Is your group or ministry an authentic community? In what stage do you think your group or ministry is in: the pseudocommunity, chaos, emptying or community stage?

- How can you lead your group through those phases in order to create authentic community?

Organizational Leadership

- Is there an avenue in your organization for people to voice their thoughts and concerns without fear of interruption or reprimand? How is this important to community building?

- What tactics can you employ to avoid burnout in the leadership of your church, organization or institution? How important is the practice of the sabbath in avoiding burnout?

- In what ways can the spiritual discipline of celebration aid in the journey toward racial reconciliation?

Prayer

Please refer to the prayer found on page 152.

Chapter 10. The Trumpet Call

Activity

Lead the group in completing the Reconciliation Generation covenant found on pages 158-59. Each member should sign it and have another member of the group witness and date it. This is a symbol of your collective accountability to the commitment to work toward racial justice and reconciliation. Invite all group members to keep and frame their copy and place it in a prominent place as a reminder to themselves of their commitment.

Discussion

Self Leadership

- Are you prepared to answer the call to racial reconciliation? Why or why not? What is hindering you? What intimidates you about making this commitment?

- Do you consider yourself to be a leader? Are you reluctant to embrace the responsibility and authority that comes with leadership?

- What will it mean for you to be a witness of racial reconciliation in your life?

Group Leadership

- As members of your group, team or ministry seek to stand in their new identity as members of the Reconciliation Generation, how can your group, team or ministry support their efforts?

- What spiritual weapons can your group, team or ministry employ collectively in the battle for racial and ethnic reconciliation?

Organizational Leadership

- How accountable is your organization or institution to the community it serves?

- How can your organization equip and prepare individuals to become agents of change in your organization or institution in order to create community?

Prayer
Please refer to the Lord's Prayer found on page 157.

CONGRATULATIONS!

You have just completed a significant and meaningful step in the journey toward racial reconciliation. You have not arrived at this benchmark alone, but you have successfully brought others with you. For this, you should certainly be commended. However, the work does not stop here. We hope that if you have learned anything, you have discovered that this process is a long and difficult one, and your journey is just beginning. Now is the time to enact those ideas, provide substance to the suggestions and, ultimately, create a place within yourself, your group, and your organization or institution for the heart of racial justice to abide, flourish and impact the nations. Godspeed as you continue your journey! Know that we will be journeying along with you and look forward to meeting you on the path.

NOTES

Chapter 1: Is There Still a Race Problem?
[1]David Frost, *Billy Graham: Personal Thoughts of a Public Man* (Colorado Springs: Chariot Victor, 1997), p. 127.
[2]Michael Emerson and Christian Smith, *Divided by Faith* (New York: Oxford University Press, 2000).

Chapter 2: Mission Impossible?
[1]Paraphrased from a conversation between Mohandas Gandhi and E. Stanley Jones. As told to Lyle Dorsett by E. Stanley Jones.

Chapter 3: A Better Way
[1]Elizabeth Y. Sung, *Culture, Race and Ethnicity in Christian Perspective: Theoretical and Theological Foundations for Multi-ethnic Ministry,* InterVarsity Christian Fellowship, 2001 (unpublished paper).
[2]For more, see Richard J. Mouw, *When the Kings Come Marching In* (Grand Rapids, Mich.: Eerdmans, 1983).

Chapter 4: A New Model
[1]Oscar Romero, *The Violence of Love,* comp. and trans. James R. Brockman (Maryknoll, N.Y.: Orbis Books, 2004).
[2]Rick spent ten years working with Leanne Payne in her Pastoral Care Ministries schools, learning to minister healing to these sexual, emotional, gender and relational areas of brokenness. We are indebted to Leanne's book *The Healing Presence* (Westchester, Ill.: Crossway, 1989) for some of the foundational insights of the healing model. Rick has also written on these issues in his forthcoming book, *Experiencing Healing Prayer* (Downers Grove, Ill.: InterVarsity Press, 2005).
[3]Sarah Hinlicky, "Talking to Generation X," *First Things* 90 (February 1999): 11.
[4]Robert Schreiter, *Reconciliation: Mission and Ministry in a Changing Social Order* (Maryknoll, N.Y.: Orbis, 1992), p. 43.
[5]Miroslav Volf, *Exclusion and Embrace: A Theological Exploration of Identity, Otherness and Reconciliation* (Nashville: Abingdon, 1996), p. 23.

[6]Schreiter, *Reconciliation,* pp. 60-61.

[7]Brother Lawrence, the medieval monk, made the expression "practice the presence of the Lord" well known. He taught that we can focus our mind and heart on the reality of God and God's constant presence with us. With that focus, we can experience the transforming power of our union with Christ in an ongoing daily way.

Chapter 5: How Worship Builds Bridges
[1]Anne Lamott, *Traveling Mercies* (New York: Anchor, 1999), pp. 47-48.

[2]Walter Brueggemann, *The Prophetic Imagination* (Philadelphia: Fortress, 1978), p. 13.

[3]Marva Dawn, *Powers, Weakness and the Tabernacling of God* (Grand Rapids, Mich.: Eerdmans, 2001), pp. 134-35.

[4]C. S. Lewis, *Mere Christianity* (New York: Macmillan, 1978), pp. 168-69.

[5]Leanne Payne, *Listening Prayer* (Grand Rapids, Mich.: Baker, 1994), pp. 236-37.

Chapter 6: Embracing Our True Selves
[1]In his forthcoming book *Experiencing Healing Prayer* (Downers Grove, Ill.: InterVarsity Press, 2005), Rick explores more fully these ideas of true self and false self.

[2]C. S. Lewis, *The Weight of Glory and Other Essays,* ed. Walter Hooper (New York: Collier, 1975), p. 18.

[3]Leanne Payne, *The Healing Presence* (Westchester, Ill.: Crossway, 1989), p. 21.

[4]Miroslav Volf, *Exclusion and Embrace: A Theological Exploration of Identity, Otherness and Reconciliation* (Nashville: Abingdon, 1996), pp. 114-16.

[5]See appendix 1's section "Race" for more on the way racial classifications developed historically.

[6]Adapted from Payne's *Healing Presence,* p. 64.

Chapter 7: Receiving and Extending Forgiveness
[1]Peggy McIntosh, "White Privilege and Male Privilege," paper, Center for Research on Women, Wellesley College, 1988, pp. 5-9.

[2]Gordon Marino, "Me? Apologize for Slavery?" *Christianity Today,* October 5, 1998, pp. 82-83.

Chapter 8: Denouncing the Powers and Principalities
[1]Marva Dawn, *Powers, Weakness and the Tabernacling of God* (Grand Rapids, Mich.: Eerdmans, 2001), p. 4.

[2]Ibid., p. 12.

[3]William Stringfellow, quoted in Bill Wylie-Kellermann, "Exorcising an American

Demon: Racism Is a Principality," *Sojourners* 27, no. 2 (1998): 16.

[4]Rick Joyner, "The Stronghold of Racism," *Morning Star Journal,* no. 5 (1991): 2.

[5]William Stringfellow, *Free in Obedience* (New York: Seabury, 1964), p. 53.

[6]Martin Luther King Jr., "Letter from Birmingham Jail," April 16, 1963, <http://almaz.com/nobel/peace/MLK-jail.html>.

[7]Bill McCartney, *Sold Out* (Nashville: Word, 1997), p. 180.

[8]Marva Dawn, *Powers, Weakness and the Tabernacling of God* (Grand Rapids, Mich.: Eerdmans, 2001), p. 47.

[9]*The Book of Common Prayer* (New York: Church Hymnal Corporation, 1979), pp. 302-3.

Chapter 9: Ongoing Partnerships

[1]Barbara Williams-Skinner, *Personal Transformation Through Reconciliation* (Tracy's Landing, Md.: Skinner Leadership Institute, 2001), p. 4.

[2]Michael Emerson and Christian Smith, *Divided by Faith* (New York: Oxford University Press, 2000), p. 171.

[3]N. K. Clifford, quoted in ibid.

[4]M. Scott Peck, *The Different Drum: Community Making and Peace* (New York: Simon & Schuster, 1987).

[5]See Rick Richardson's book *Evangelism Outside the Box* (Downers Grove, Ill.: InterVarsity Press, 2000) to explore evangelism in a postmodern culture. Rick looks at how for postmodern people, experience comes before explanation, image comes before word, and belonging comes before believing.

[6]Written by David Mange and Marc Papai of InterVarsity Christian Fellowship.

Appendix 1: Definitions

[1]Lausanne Committee on World Evangelization, "A Definition of Culture" in *The Willowbank Report* (LCWE, 1978), <http://www.gospelcom.net/lcwe/LOP/lop02.htm#2>.

[2]Max Weber, *Economy and Society* (New York: Bedminster Press, 1968), 1:389.

[3]Victoria Neufeldt, ed., *Webster's New World Dictionary,* 3rd college ed. (New York: Simon & Schuster, 1988), p. 1106.

[4]Paul Salopek, "Basically, We Are All the Same," *Chicago Tribune,* April 27, 1997, p. 10.

[5]Douglas R. Sharp. *No Partiality: The Idolatry of Race and the New Humanity* (Downers Grove, Ill.: InterVarsity Press, 2002), pp. 44-45.

[6]Michael Emerson and Christian Smith, *Divided by Faith* (New York: Oxford University Press, 2000), p. 7.

[7]Quoted in ibid., p. 9

Appendix 3: The Principalities and Powers

[1]Robert Linthicum, *City of God, City of Satan* (Grand Rapids, Mich.: Zondervan, 1991), p. 75.

[2]Marva Dawn, *Powers, Weakness, and the Tabernacling of God* (Grand Rapids, Mich.: Eerdmans, 2001), p. 22.

[3]Ibid., p. 31.

[4]Ibid., p. 47.

BIBLIOGRAPHY

The Book of Common Prayer. New York: Oxford University Press, 1990.

Brueggemann, Walter. *The Prophetic Imagination.* Philadelphia: Fortress, 1978.

Dawn, Marva. *Powers, Weakness and the Tabernacling of God.* Grand Rapids, Mich.: Eerdmans, 2001.

Dawson, John. *Healing America's Wounds.* Ventura, Calif.: Regal, 1994.

————. *Taking Our Cities for God: How to Break Spiritual Strongholds.* Lake Mary, Fla.: Creation House, 1989.

Ellis, Carl F., Jr. *Beyond Liberation: The Gospel in the Black American Experience.* Downers Grove, Ill.: InterVarsity Press, 1983.

Emerson, Michael, and Christian Smith. *Divided by Faith.* New York: Oxford University Press, 2000.

Gates, Henry Louis, Jr. *Race, Writing and Difference.* Chicago: University of Chicago Press, 1986.

Hazen-Hammond, Susan. *Timelines of Native American History.* New York: Berkeley Publishing Group, 1997.

Hinlicky, Sarah. "Talking to Generation X." *First Things* 90 (February 1999): 11.

Joyner, Rick. "The Stronghold of Racism." *Morning Star Journal,* no. 5 (1991): 2-7.

King, Martin Luther, Jr. *Strength to Love.* Philadelphia: Fortress, 1963.

Kivel, Paul. *Uprooting Racism: How White People Can Work for Racial Justice.* Gabriola Island, B.C., Canada: New Society, 1996.

Lamott, Anne. *Traveling Mercies: Some Thoughts on Faith.* New York: Anchor, 1999.

Lausanne Committee on World Evangelization. *The Willowbank Report.* LCWE, 1978, <http://www.gospelcom.net/lcwe/LOP/lop02.htm#2>.

Lewis, C. S. *Mere Christianity.* San Francisco: Harper & Row, 1980.

————. *The Weight of Glory and Other Essays.* Edited by Walter Hooper. New York: Collier, 1975.

Lewis, John. *Walking with the Wind: A Memoir of the Movement.* New York: Simon & Schuster, 1998.

Linthicum, Robert C. *City of God, City of Satan.* Grand Rapids, Mich.: Zondervan, 1991.

Malcolm X and Alex Haley. *The Autobiography of Malcolm X.* New York: Ballantine Books, 1992.

Marino, Gordon. "Me? Apologize for Slavery?" *Christianity Today,* October 5, 1998.

McCartney, Bill. *Sold Out.* Nashville: Word, 1997.

McIntosh, Peggy. "White Privilege and Male Privilege." Paper. Center for Research on Women, Wellesley College, 1988. A short version focusing on white privilege is available at <http://www.utoronto.ca/acc/events/peggy1.htm>.

Mouw, Richard J. *When the Kings Come Marching In.* Grand Rapids, Mich.: Eerdmans, 1983.

Novas, Himilce. *Everything You Need to Know About Latino History.* New York: Plume, 1994.

Payne, Leanne. *The Healing Presence.* Westchester, Ill.: Crossway, 1989.

Peck, M. Scott. *The Different Drum: Community Making and Peace.* New York: Simon & Schuster, 1987.

Perkins, Spencer, and Chris Rice. *More Than Equals: Racial Healing for the Sake of the Gospel.* Downers Grove, Ill.: InterVarsity Press, 1993.

Raybon, Patricia. *My First White Friend: Confessions on Race, Love and Forgiveness.* New York: Penguin, 1997.

Rivers, Eugene F. "Blocking the Prayers of the Church: The Idol of White Supremacy." *Sojourners* 26, no. 2 (1997): 26-31.

Salopek, Paul. "Basically, We Are All the Same." *Chicago Tribune,* April 27, 1997, pp. 10-11.

Schreiter, Robert J. *Reconciliation: Mission and Ministry in a Changing Social Order.* Maryknoll, N.Y.: Orbis, 1992.

———. *The Spirituality of Reconciliation.* Maryknoll, N.Y.: Orbis, 1998.

Sharp, Douglas R. *No Partiality: The Idolatry of Race and the New Humanity,* Downers Grove, Ill.: InterVarsity Press, 2002.

Stringfellow, William. *An Ethic for Christians and Other Aliens in a Strange Land.* Waco, Tex.: Word, 1973.

———. *Free in Obedience.* New York: Seabury, 1964.

———. *My People Is the Enemy.* New York: Holt, Rinehart and Winston, 1964.

Sung, Elizabeth Y. "Culture, Race and Ethnicity in Christian Perspective: Theoretical and Theological Foundations for Multi-ethnic Ministry." InterVarsity Christian Fellowship, 2001.

Takaki, Ronald. *Strangers from a Different Shore.* Rev. ed. Boston: Little, Brown, 1998.

Tutu, Desmond. *Hope and Suffering.* Grand Rapids, Mich.: Eerdmans, 1983.

———. *No Future Without Forgiveness.* New York: Doubleday, 1999.

Twiss, Richard. *One Church, Many Tribes: Following Jesus the Way God Made You.* San Francisco: Regal, 2000.

Volf, Miroslav. *Exclusion and Embrace: A Theological Exploration of Identity, Otherness and Reconciliation.* Nashville: Abingdon, 1996.

Weber, Max. *Economy and Society.* Berkeley: University of California Press, 1968.

Williams-Skinner, Barbara, *Personal Transformation Through Reconciliation.* Tracy's Landing, Md.: Skinner Leadership Institute, 2001.

Wink, Walter. *Engaging the Powers: Discernment and Resistance in a World of Domination.* Minneapolis: Fortress, 1992.

———. *The Powers That Be: Theology for a New Millennium.* New York: Doubleday, 1987.

Wylie-Kellermann, Bill. "Exorcising an American Demon: Racism Is a Principality." *Sojourners,* 27, no. 2 (1998): 16-20.

Yancey, George. *One Body, One Spirit: Principles of Successful Multiracial Churches.* Downers Grove, Ill.: InterVarsity Press, 2003.

RECOMMENDED RESOURCES

Movies and Educational Videos

The following movies and videos provocatively address issues of race, privilege and power. In some cases the material is adult oriented, so discretion should be exercised when using these materials with children and students. Many of the films can be obtained from the Mennonite Central Committee Video Library, 717-859-1151.

A Class Divided: Brown Eyes, Blue Eyes

The Color of Fear, Stir Fry Video Productions

Cry, the Beloved Country

Do the Right Thing, directed by Spike Lee

Eyes on the Prize video series

500 Nations video series

The Joy Luck Club

Mi Familia

El Norte

Rosewood

Smoke Signals

A Time to Kill

White Man's Burden

Books

Emerson, Michael O., and Christian Smith. *Divided by Faith: Evangelical Religion and the Problem of Race in America.* New York: Oxford University Press, 2000.

Foster, Charles R., and Theodore Brelsford. *We Are the Church Together: Cultural Diversity in Congregational Life.* Valley Forge, Penn.: Trinity Press, 1996.

Hazen-Hammond, Susan. *Timelines of Native American History.* New York:

Berkeley Publishing Group, 1997.

Hines, S. G., and Curtiss P. DeYoung. *Beyond Rhetoric: Reconciliation as a Way of Life*. Valley Forge, Penn.: Judson, 2000.

Lewis, John. *Walking with the Wind: A Memoir of the Movement*. New York: Simon & Schuster, 1998.

Malcolm X and Alex Haley. *The Autobiography of Malcolm X*. New York: Ballantine Books, 1992.

Matsuoka, Fumitaka. *The Color of Faith: Building Community in a Multiracial Society*. Cleveland: United Church Press, 1998.

Novas, Himilce. *Everything You Need to Know About Latino History*. New York: Plume, 2003.

Ortiz, Manuel. *One New People: Models for Developing a Multiethnic Church*. Downers Grove, Ill.: InterVarsity Press, 1996.

Raybon, Patricia. *My First White Friend: Confessions on Race, Love and Forgiveness*. New York: Penguin, 1997.

Rhodes, Stephen A. *Where the Nations Meet: The Church in a Multicultural World*. Downers Grove, Ill.: InterVarsity Press, 1998.

Schreiter, Robert J. *The Ministry of Reconciliation: Spirituality and Strategies*. Maryknoll, N.Y.: Orbis, 2000.

Sung Park, Andrew. *Racial Conflict and Healing: An Asian-American Perspective*. New York: Orbis, 1996.

Takaki, Ronald. *Strangers from a Different Shore*. Rev. ed. Boston: Little, Brown, 1998.

Toussaint, Pamela, and Jo Kadlecek. *I Call You Friend: Four Women's Stories of Race, Faith and Friendship*. Nashville: Broadman and Holman, 1999.

Twiss, Richard. *One Church, Many Tribes: Following Jesus the Way God Made You*. San Francisco: Regal, 2000.

Woodley, Randy. *Living in Color: Embracing God's Passion for Diversity*. Grand Rapids, Mich.: Chosen Books, 2001.

Yancey, George. *One Body, One Spirit: Principles of Successful Multiracial Churches*. Downers Grove, Ill.: InterVarsity Press, 2003.